Innovation in Silicon Valley

(Leadership with freedom)

Diego F. Wartjes

Innovation in Silicon Valley
(Leadership with freedom)
Copyright © 2024 Diego F. Wartjes
ISBN-13: 9798332889738
First edition: July 2024
Translation from Spanish into English by Edward Green, Buenos Aires

This book is dedicated to Stanford professor **Robert I. Sutton**, from whom I learned what innovation is and how to promote it.

Diego F. Wartjes

Index

CHAPTER 1 .... **11**
INNOVATION IN SILICON VALLEY **11**
    LEADERSHIP IN SILICON VALLEY 14
    WHAT IS SILICON VALLEY? 17

CHAPTER 2 .... **23**
INNOVATION AND CREATIVITY **23**
    PERSEVERANCE IS DECISIVE 24
    WHAT IS CREATIVITY? 25
    TECHNOLOGICAL AND SCIENTIFIC REVOLUTIONS 27
    HENRY FORD: THE ASSEMBLY LINE AND CATTLE SLAUGHTERHOUSES 29
    THE GENETIC REVOLUTION AND EINSTEIN'S THEORIES 31
    THE INTERSECTION BETWEEN ART AND TECHNOLOGY 32
    DIFFERENT WAYS OF SEEING THE SAME THING 34
    ROUTINE WORK AND INNOVATIVE WORK 36
    MANY ATTEMPTS TO ACHIEVE AN INNOVATIVE PRODUCT 37
    FAILURE DOES NOT EXIST 38
    THE CREATIVE PROCESS 39

CHAPTER 3 .... **43**
ENTREPRENEURIAL CAPITALISM AND THE SKILLS OF INNOVATORS **43**
    KNOWLEDGE, VISION AND CAPITAL FOR ENTREPRENEURS 45
    THE CREATIVE SKILLS OF INNOVATORS 49
    QUESTIONING 51
    OBSERVING 52
    EXPERIMENTING 55
    NETWORKING 58
    PRACTICING CREATIVE SKILLS 60
    SOME MEASURES TO PROMOTE A CULTURE OF INNOVATION 63
    NEVER GIVE UP 67

CHAPTER 4 71
WHAT DOES BEING A "GOOD BOSS" MEAN? 71

- Psychological safety 74
- Psychological safety in Google teams 77
- Power distance and individualism 79
- Being in tune with the people you lead 88
- The cookie experiment 90
- The small steps strategy 92
- Protect their backs 94
- The use of time in meetings 96

CHAPTER 5 99
COLLABORATION WITHIN THE TEAM 99

- The *T-Shape* people concept 102
- Obstacles to collaboration 103
- The silo mentality 105
- Incentives for collaboration 107
- A mix of novices and experts 108
- Combining delivery and creative skills 110
- The ideal number of members in a team 113
- Negativism in the team 116
- The bad is stronger than the good 118

CHAPTER 6 121
BELIEVE IN THE IMPOSSIBLE 121

- The role of critical members 122
- "Optimistic but concerned" members 123
- Does money encourage creativity? 124
- Money and the passion to innovate 126
- Autonomy fosters enthusiasm 128
- The case of the MSN Encarta encyclopedia (Microsoft) .. 130
- Constructive conflicts 131
- How to motivate the team. The role of emotions 135
- Strategies to motivate 137

CHAPTER 7 141
IMPLEMENTATION 141

- Measures to counteract the "smart talk trap" 142

Three final tips	146
CHAPTER 8	**151**
WHAT IS IDEO?	**151**
The 6 attributes of the most innovative companies in the world	155
CONCLUSION	**165**
INNOVATION LEADERSHIP IN THE 21ST CENTURY	**165**
REFERENCE LIST	**171**
Books	171
Articles, studies (journals), papers, and interviews	175
FOOTNOTES	**197**

> Management is about persuading people to do things they do not want to do, while leadership is about inspiring people to do things they never thought they could.[1]
>
> Steve Jobs

Chapter 1

Innovation in Silicon Valley

This book is called Innovation in Silicon Valley for two reasons. First, it describes the innovative vision of young entrepreneurs in Silicon Valley. It differs greatly from the traditional vision of innovation that generally believes that only large companies (especially manufacturing industries) or governments can generate innovation with the assistance of their *research* and *development* departments, while their clients are often other organisations. For example, IBM's manufacture of large computers (the so-called *mainframes*) for banks, companies and governments in the 1950s and 1960s.[2] Their management style is traditional or hierarchical and if an entrepreneur or work group is unable to create the proposed innovative product, it constitutes a failure. That is why many executives see innovation projects or trying something new as putting their careers at risk, more so because of the low probability of success. A research and development effort that achieves nothing or wastes money is rarely forgotten and can mean dismissal for the person in charge or a denied promotion.

Instead, like-minded innovators in Silicon Valley and elsewhere developed a new way to innovate. They believe that it is the *individuals* who can create the most disruptive innovations, working on their laptops. An example is Mark Zuckerberg who developed Facebook in his room at Harvard University or Elon Musk and his partners creating PayPal. With the invention of the *microchip*, the personal computer and software, tools became available to create other products for *individual* use, from programs such as Windows 95 by Microsoft (its first office opened in Silicon Valley in 1981) or QuickBooks (accounting software for small family businesses) to social networks that run on the Internet such as Yahoo, Google, YouTube, Twitter, LinkedIn, Whatsapp, Airbnb, Instagram, Pinterest, Reddit, OpenAI, AddLive, Snapchat, Meerkat, Zynga, Nextdoor, and so on. Take LinkedIn, Facebook and Instagram today allowing millions of people to massively disseminate their ideas, work achievements or concerns. In the past, they could only do this if they were interviewed on radio or television.

They are the protagonists of *entrepreneurial capitalism*, which stands out for innovating regardless of the resources at their disposal: Steve Jobs and Steve Wozniak had nothing when they founded Apple, they sold some of their most valuable personal possessions to get their first dollars. These entrepreneurs have foolproof perseverance. For them, technological products had to be not only useful but also beautiful (artistic), as can be seen today in the colourful design of Internet pages, the stylish design of computers or the beauty of the latest *iPhone* (Jobs was obsessed with the intersection of art and technology). According to Vivek Wadhwa (Singularity University),

> Here people understand that through each failure you have learned something, and that therefore you are wiser than before. There is a very different culture from that of most countries in the world and much of the United States. In New York, bankers wear suits and ties and brag about their successes, real or imagined. Here, in Silicon Valley, the richest businessmen and the most prestigious scientists walk around in jeans, or shorts and sandals, and talk *matter-of-factly about their failures*. It's another world.[3]

They also believe that the main customers should be other individuals, the "common man in the street." In effect, this type of entrepreneur managed to make available to individuals the technologies that had been created for large companies and governments. We forget that the first radios, calculators, computers, printers, photocopiers, floppy disks and, recently, 3D printers, were bulky and expensive. They had not been designed for personal use and were not adapted for that purpose until the arrival of this generation of entrepreneurs. Take the first computer, the Eniac, in 1946; it weighed 30 tons and took up a floor space of 15 by 10 meters.

For many years manufacturers of large computers neglected the individual and produced only for companies, banks and governments. But Apple, Commodore, Tandy and, beginning in 1981, IBM focused on making computers for personal use and thus created individual computing markets.[4] Hewlett-Packard sold a sophisticated laser printer at a price of 100 thousand dollars. But in 1984 it launched the first personal ink jet printer (HP ThinkJet) for only $495 and thus created a market for students and office workers (over 400 million of these printers were sold). The Internet is also today for personal use thanks to the fact that some of the scientists who built it distrusted the US government. One of these scientists, Bob Taylor, stated,

> Whenever possible, I chose to decentralize the network (...) I did not trust large, centralized organizations.[5]

And if we review history, we will remember that radios were large devices for shared use that were placed in the living room or kitchen of the home. In the 1950s, making a small portable radio was revolutionary. But one innovator, Pat Haggerty (Texas Instruments), asked his people to make a small pocket radio, the Regency TR-1, which came on the market in 1954 at a price of $49.95. It was an absolute success. One hundred thousand were sold in one year, making it one of the most popular innovations in history. The radio was no longer a large device that had to be shared with the rest of the family but rather a personal device that allowed each individual to listen to the music or program of their choice.

In the 1990s, Harvard Professor Clayton Christensen called these innovations "disruptive technologies" to differentiate them from "sustainable technologies" – those characterized by improving the performance of "established products." The "disruptive technology" innovations are typically "cheaper, simpler, smaller and, frequently, more convenient to use", ideal for individuals. The examples Christensen gave in 1997 were the small Honda motorcycles versus the large Harley-Davidson motorcycles, and small transistors versus vacuum tubes.[6] This is how electronic technology ceased to be the exclusive domain of large companies and the American government, to "empower individuality, personal freedom and even –to a certain extent– rebellious spirit" said Walter Isaacson.[7]

Leadership in Silicon Valley

Second, the subtitle of this book is *Leadership with freedom*. Why is this? For a group of people to manage to innovate, leadership is decisive; the example set by leaders like Steve Jobs or Bill Gates is enough. There are many ways to lead, but the leadership style that this book describes emerged in Silicon Valley, one that many management professors recommend as ideal for fostering creativity. To capture its essence, we will look at several topics: the creative skills of famous innovators such as Pierre Omidyar (eBay) or Jeff Bezos (Amazon); the degree of influence of positive, negative or neutral emotions in the company environment; the discoveries of the consulting firm IDEO (which Steve Jobs used to consult), the ideal number of members in an innovation team (type of personalities that need to be combined) and much more. Without knowing these topics, a boss or manager would not know where to start to lead an innovation team. Let us delve deeper into the concept of leadership with freedom.

In the 1940s and 1960s, this leadership style was created by two entrepreneurs, David Packard, co-founder of Hewlett-Packard (1939) and Robert Noyce, co-founder of Intel (1968) and inventor of the microchip.[8] For inventing the microchip, Noyce was nicknamed the "mayor of Silicon Valley" until his death in 1990. His companies were the most iconic in Silicon Valley until the emergence of Apple in 1976, then Google (1998) and Facebook (2004). During World War II (1939-1945), Packard would often sleep in his office from where he supervised several shifts of workers, mostly of women. He realized, according to Isaacson, that giving workers flexible schedules and freedom in deciding how to meet their goals increased efficiency (at this time his partner, Bill Hewlett, was in the army). Added to this was the Californian lifestyle with its sunny climate, beer-drinking outings at the end of the day (happy hour) and stock options for workers, which encouraged their commitment: if the company increased its profits, so did the share price.

Noyce also believed in giving workers freedom to make decisions and come up with ingenious solutions. Under this type of management that some call "horizontal," good ideas spread more quickly, different from what happens under hierarchical or authoritarian ("vertical") leadership. Ted Hoff, one of the Intel technicians who invented the microprocessor in 1971, recalls that Intel staff were not required to follow the chain of command. If an employee needed to speak to a manager or director, they did so without having to ask permission from intermediaries, supervisors, or secretaries. By circumventing the hierarchical structure, Noyce empowered Intel's young people, forcing them to become creative. He was convinced that if you chose the right person for a task, you didn't need to keep an eye on them.[9]

He had developed this leadership style after being held back by the rigid hierarchy of a company he had worked for as a young man. In companies in eastern United States (New York, New Jersey, Connecticut, Massachusetts, etc.), lower-ranking workers had small metal desks while executives had huge mahogany ones, a symbol of hierarchical command. So Noyce decided to work at a small grey desk in the centre of the room, so everyone could see and access him easily. Journalist Michael Malone said, after visiting Intel,

I wasn't able to locate Noyce. A secretary had to get up and take me to his cubicle, because it was almost indistinguishable from the rest in that extensive meadow of cubicles.[10]

There were therefore no better desks for bosses, nor any reserved parking places. What was the aim of this "desk equality"? Not to preach egalitarian socialism or Marxism, but to point to the fact that the hierarchy of the position and its privileges had to yield to good ideas and merits. According to Ann Bowers, Intel's chief people officer,

> There were no privileges. We promoted a type of company culture completely different from anything that had been seen before. It was a culture based on meritocracy.[11]

This leadership style "was to become a common model in Silicon Valley."[12] Steve Jobs idolized Noyce and this is how he remembers him: "Noyce took me under his wing. I was young, in my twenties. He was in his early fifties and tried to give me a perspective on the industry that I only partially understood."[13] In an interview shortly before dying, Jobs was asked if he always imposed his ideas because of his hierarchy.

> I wish I had. You can't. If you want to hire talented people and have them stay working for you, you have to let them make many decisions and let the good ideas win, not hierarchy: the best ideas have to win, otherwise, the talented people leave you.[14]

Many business professors call this form of leadership "laissez-faire management"[15] and others use the word *freedom* to describe its essence. Stanford University Professor Thomas Byers comments,

> Many of the most successful and innovative companies consist of small business units with freedom of communication between them ... and freedom from centralized micro-management.[16]

It is no coincidence that this vision has emerged in the United States, a country with the highest degree of economic freedom in history, despite the high taxes that today govern Silicon Valley and the rest of California. Thurman John "T. J." Rodgers, founder of Cypress Semiconductor (Apple supplier), stated that,

> It is the American freedom that allows Silicon Valley to exist. Liberty and free markets are embodied in our Constitution and Bill of Rights. Freedom creates prosperity. Silicon Valley is an island of freedom and free markets, more in line with the laissez-faire philosophy of 1776 than with the United States of 1999 and its state interventionism.[17]

What is Silicon Valley?

To conclude this introduction, here are some more facts about Silicon Valley. It is not a city or municipality, but a *region* (a geographic area) located in the north of the state of California (south of San Francisco). The region includes 13 cities, of which the most famous, due to the companies residing there, are San José (home of eBay and Cisco), Cupertino (Apple), Palo Alto (Hewlett-Packard and Tesla), Mountain View (Google), Santa Clara (Nvidia), etc. (technically the city of San Francisco is not part of Silicon Valley according to the Silicon Valley Chamber of Commerce).[18] It is called Silicon for the manufacturing process of *silicon* microchips and *Valley* for the Santa Clara Valley. The name "Silicon Valley" was first used by journalist Don Hoefler in 1971 in a series of articles published in *Electronic News* magazine.

There are approximately 2,000 software, social media, laser, fibre optic, robotics and medical instrument companies: Apple, Google, Facebook, eBay, LinkedIn, Adobe, Intel, Cisco, Netflix, Nvidia, Paypal, Oracle, Zoom, Visa, Tesla, SAP, Xerox, DuPont, etc. Between mid-2020 and mid-2021, almost 79,000 jobs were created. Of the 583,300 tech jobs in Silicon Valley and San Francisco, 38% (219,000 people) are with one of the region's 25 largest tech companies. Google and Apple are the largest employers, of about 7% and 6%, respectively, followed by Facebook (3%), Cisco (2%) and Amazon (2%).

More than a third of the 141 North American, European and Asian companies that achieved a value of more than $1 billion –between 2010 and 2015– have offices in Silicon Valley; 61 percent of companies with innovation centres have a presence there.[19] The entrepreneurs of this place were decisive in promoting the *Third Industrial Revolution* with the invention of the microchip and the personal computer, which together with the internet have brought about the *Fourth Industrial Revolution* we are experiencing today: artificial intelligence, drones, driverless cars, robotics, genetics, nanotechnology, *big data*, etc. It is recognized for attracting the best engineers in the world, especially from India and China: between 1995 and 2005 more than half of its new companies were founded by immigrants. Satya Nadella and Sundar Pichai were born in India and are the CEOs, respectively, of Microsoft and Google. Without immigration freedom, Silicon Valley would not be what it is. However, many American politicians only think about banning it or putting up obstacles.[20]

In the history of this place, Stanford University holds a prominent position since the first message on ARPAnet (today's Internet) was sent from the University of California to Stanford University in 1969. Much of the knowledge in this book comes from this university located in the heart of Silicon Valley (Palo Alto) – perhaps the best in the world for learning innovation. Stanford professors (from whom I learned in their classes) give seminars and innovation courses to executives working for companies located in Silicon Valley. As many as 20 Nobel Prize winners (as of 2023) teach at Stanford and it competes with Harvard and M.I.T. in the best international rankings. It is known for its culture of companies and "start-ups" and, according to some, "it is an unwritten rule that to be a successful professor at Stanford you must open a company."[21] An engineering professor, Fred Terman (1900-1982), who encouraged his students in the 1930s to open electronic products companies, had a lot to do with this. Terman took his students to visit technology companies and lent $500 to Stanford students William Hewlett and David Packard to start the Hewlett-

Packard computer company in 1939. In the early 1950s, Terman, now as dean of the university, promoted the opening of an industrial park (Stanford Research Park) and encouraged technology companies to settle there to collaborate with university professors and students. By 1960, more than 40 companies had set up shop in this park. Terman had a lot of faith in technology:

> Almost everything one wants to do in this world today is either possible or can be done better with electronics. With its ability to control, amplify and convert into light, sound or electricity, it is the nervous system for our machine civilization.[22]

Today Google, Tesla, SAP, Xerox, DuPont, and 150 more companies have facilities in this park. Companies founded by Stanford professors and students include Google, Netflix, Instagram, Hewlett-Packard, eBay, Yahoo, Gap, Taiwan Semiconductor, Charles Schwab Corp., IDEO, Nike, Logitech, Tesla Motors, Cisco Systems, Sun Microsystems, PayPal and LinkedIn. Among its inventors are the creator of the internet protocol, Vinton Cerf (one of the "fathers" of the internet), Ted Maiman who invented the first laser, Brad Parkinson, the inventor of GPS and Blake Ross, who created the Mozilla Firefox program. A 2012 study estimated that companies founded by students and professors from this university generate annual profits of 2.7 trillion dollars and have created some 5.4 million jobs since 1930. The graduates from this university have set up approximately 40,000 companies which, if placed in an independent nation, would make up the *tenth economy in the world*. The economy of the state of California is the sixth in the world.[23] Many famous athletes have been part of Stanford teams, for example, golfer Tiger Woods and tennis player John McEnroe, both former world number 1. Steve Jobs gave a memorable speech to Stanford students in 2005. He said: "The only way to do great work is to *love what you do*. If you haven't found it yet, keep looking."

In 2021, more than half of new invention patents in California (52%) were registered in the name of Silicon Valley inventors. Since 1990, its patents —out of all those in the United States— have increased from 4% to 12%, despite having less than 1% of the country's population. The number of patents doubled between 2009 and 2020, reaching a record of 21,770 registered patents.[24] Despite pandemic restrictions, companies in Silicon Valley and San Francisco reached 14 *trillion* dollars (twelve zeros) in market value while the *venture capital* that finances entrepreneurs reached an all-time high of 95 billion dollars in 2021 (compared to $131.8 billion in the entire state of California and $272 billion in the United States as a whole).

This capital attracted 230 unicorns (these are start-up companies worth, at least, 1 billion dollars). Silicon Valley is synonymous with *creativity* and *venture capital* and that is why some compare it to Florence during the Renaissance, given that this Italian city also had these elements: the creativity of Leonardo Da Vinci or Filippo Brunelleschi and the capital of bankers such as the Medici family. Steve Jobs idolized Leonardo: "He saw beauty in art and engineering and his ability to combine them made him a genius."[25]

People working in Silicon Valley and San Francisco on average have a much higher level of education than in California or the United States as a whole, with bachelor's, master's, or doctor's degrees. 39% of Silicon Valley's population are foreign-born, a much higher proportion than that of the state of California (26%) or the United States as a whole (13%). Average salaries are much higher in Silicon Valley and San Francisco (USD 169,900 and USD 173,000 respectively) than in California (USD 89,200) and the United States (USD 71,700) –at 2021 values. Of the 141,000 millionaires in Silicon Valley (those with more than $1 million in assets), an estimated 6,900 have more than $10 million.[26] Due to all this, a recent study ranks Silicon Valley as the first innovation ecosystem in the world. As a consultant says: "Never has so much wealth been created in such a short time by so few people."[27]

However, entrepreneurs also donate millions of dollars to charities and for other social purposes. Silicon Valley is home to nearly 1,000 foundations that hold a total of $72 billion in assets. In fiscal year 2019-2020, the top 50 philanthropists (entrepreneurs) donated $225 million, about $43 million more than the previous year thanks to increases by Cisco (+15.6 million), Google (+6 million), Wells Fargo (+3.6 million) among others. The largest local donor among the top 50 corporate philanthropists for the 2019-20 fiscal year was the *Sobrato Philanthropies Foundation* ($63.4 million).[28]

For more than 65 years, the Sobrato family has been developing the real estate business for companies (e.g. the former Apple campus, Netflix offices, etc.) and family communities in Silicon Valley. They have also donated money to countless educational projects. One of these projects teaches English to Spanish-speaking children (Latin American immigrants). Entrepreneur and founder, John Sobrato, said,

> I truly believe that education is the surest way out of poverty. We have been very involved in schools. It's something I enjoy doing and it's great to see these kids move forward.[29]

The following are the 15 largest donors (businessmen), in millions of dollars.

COMPANIES	DONATION
Sobrato Philanthropies	$ 63.4
Cisco Systems	$ 45.6
Alphabet/Google	$ 28.9
Wells Fargo Bank	$ 9.04
KLA Corp	$ 8.5
SAP	$ 8.19
Applied Materials	$ 7.34
Gilead Sciences	$ 4.89
Nvidia	$ 4.89
Intel	$ 4.58
Adobe	$ 4.52
Bank of America	$ 4.34
Silicon Valley Bank	$ 2.74
Micron Technology	$ 2.2
eBay	$ 2.1

DIEGO F. WARTJES

Bill Gates surpasses them all in the amount of millions donated though he lives not in Silicon Valley but in Seattle, Washington state, where Microsoft has its headquarters. Therefore, he is not included in this ranking. Having completed this introduction, we enter fully into the exciting world of innovation.

> Genius is 1% inspiration and 99% perspiration. [30]
>
> **Thomas Edison**

Chapter 2

Innovation and creativity

It is essential to distinguish creativity from innovation, two concepts that are often confused. Innovation is a combination of two concepts: i) creativity and ii) implementation. This clarification is important because thousands of executives have been surveyed and, in general, they believe that creativity is innovation. But innovation is not creativity. Creativity is just the beginning: it is having a good idea but if not implemented, there is no innovation. That's why Bill Gates says "I'll pay a dollar for your good idea and a million if you can implement it."[31] Implementation is the hardest part. There are those who say that "we lack good ideas" but facts show that what is lacking is implementation. The reason why many companies have "stumbled" or fallen behind is not because they did not have ideas or did not know what was coming in their industry, but because they lacked the implementation, the development of the idea.

Kodak, for example, knew that digital photography was going to dominate the market. In fact it was a Kodak engineer, Steve Sasson, who invented the digital camera in 1975, long before the digital era. Looking back on this project, many didn't realize it was the world's first digital camera, including Sasson himself.[32] This company has more many patents in digital photography. But for many Kodak executives, going digital meant ending the film business —the goose that laid the golden egg. Hewlett & Packard had an e-reader several years before Amazon's Kindle (2007) or Apple's iPad (2010). Edison's light bulb was an idea that had been around for 40 years but it was Edison who implemented it. In these cases, the ideas were there. It was the implementation that was needed.

In a survey, a group of executives were asked to rate from 1 to 10 their companies' ability to generate ideas (creativity) and their ability to implement them. Executives responded that their companies are better at generating ideas (average score of 6) than at implementing them, average score of 1. According to studies, proposing ideas is common among executives for two reasons: first, it does not create any tension with their company's business and second it looks good. The executive looks like a "smart guy" while implementation is long, laborious and requires resources.[33]

Perseverance is decisive

Coming up with some good ideas is not as difficult as many believe. If a work team devotes ten hours a day for a week to generating ideas, it will eventually come up with some good idea. However, the biggest difficulty is finding the right people to make it a reality and transform it into a successful business. This is why professors with a lot of experience in the world of innovation say that ideas are not scarce, what is scarce are people with *perseverance, determination and experience to implement them*.[34] And that is why great innovators put more emphasis on perseverance than on creativity. Steve Jobs: "I am convinced that approximately half of what separates successful entrepreneurs from unsuccessful ones is merely perseverance..."[35] The thing about innovative products is that they dazzle when you see them and that makes many forget the effort that was required to make them.

Silicon Valley's top investors and venture capital funds emphasize the importance of people over ideas when deciding which entrepreneurs to lend money to. Why is this? Because if the idea is wrong but people have the ability and the perseverance, they can change the idea – *pivot,* in entrepreneurs' jargon – but if people lack these skills, not much can be done. Arthur Rock earned more than a billion dollars investing in Intel and Apple and always stressed that he invested "in people, not ideas. If you can find capable people who are wrong about the product, they will change it…" Likewise, investor John Doerr of the famous Kleiner Perkins fund who bet on Amazon and Google always looks first at the biographies of the team members.[36] In short, there are many people with novel ideas but few with the capacity and perseverance to implement them. Starting new things and overcoming obstacles requires skills that can be found in "a small fraction of the population."[37]

What is creativity?

Sometimes, when people hear the word creativity and think of Steve Jobs or Jeff Bezos, they believe that only this kind of people can be creative. But something that can help lose one's fear of creativity, says professor Robert Sutton (Stanford), is to understand what it consists of. Basically it is combining *existing materials but in new ways* or, a variant of this, *taking existing ideas from one industry to create products in another.* An example of combining existing things to create a new product is the *wheeled luggage bag.* The wheel has existed since approximately 3,500 years before Christ and suitcases already existed in the 19th century – strictly speaking, they were trunks back then – but it was not until 1972 that someone – Bernard Sadow – thought of combining these two to make suitcases with wheels. One day, while carrying two suitcases with his wife at an airport, upon returning from a vacation in Aruba, he observed a worker effortlessly moving a heavy machine on a roller skate. So he said to his wife, "That's what we need for our luggage."[38] When he returned to work, he pulled some wheels out of a closet, tied a strap to the suitcase, pulled, and it worked.

This invention earned him patent no. 3,653,474 but it was not a financial success. The successful one was the Rollaboard suitcase, invented in 1987 by Robert Plath, a Northwest Airlines 747 pilot who fitted two wheels and a long handle to his suitcases. These rolled in an upright position, instead of horizontally like Sadow's four-wheel model. Within a few years, Plath stopped flying to found Travelpro International, a major luggage company. Other luggage manufacturers quickly imitated the Rollaboard model. Another example of combining existing materials to create a new product is the *Comotomo* bottle, from which babies suck to drink milk. The spout and body are made of silicone, resembling the softness of a mother's breast.

It is the best rated by mothers in the United States but it is just the combination of things that have existed for decades – the milk bottle and silicone – only that no one had thought of merging them. Economist Xavier Sala-i-Martin had the iPhone 5S pulverized with a hammer to turn it into dust: the largest pile of dust was lithium (about 30 grams), then there were 27 grams of plastic, 20 grams of glass, 16 grams of copper, 15 grams of chromium, 14 grams of aluminium, 0.00034 grams of gold and 0.00034 of platinum. If you were to take these powders to the market, they could sell for as little as $2. But when creatively combined, these materials make up a cell phone worth more than $600.[39]

An example of taking ideas that already exist in one market to create new products in another is plasticine –that soft malleable dough that children use to knead and create figures that comes in various colours. In the 1950s Joe McVicker had a plant in Cincinnati that produced a paste to clean soot residue from walls from coal heating. But after World War II, with the shift from coal to natural gas heating, demand for his product declined sharply. One day his sister-in-law who lived in New York – Kay Zufall – stopped by McVicker's house and since she was a kindergarten teacher and was always looking for something to entertain children with, she took a jar of the paste to see if the children liked it. She also used it to make little stars and birds that she hung from her Christmas tree. When McVicker saw these figures hanging from the Zufall tree, he was impressed by how easy it was to mould the dough. At Zufall's suggestion, McVicker reformulated the product by adding colour to make it more attractive to children. And so Plasticine was born. Zufall and her husband Bob named it Play-Doh and with McVicker created one of the most successful products of all time, having sold more than 2 billion jars of play dough since 1956. [40] In 2003, the Toy Industry Association added Play-Doh to their list of the 100 most creative toys of the century.

Taking ideas from one industry to create new products in another is the "plastic valve" of those water bottles that athletes use to hydrate, says Sutton in *Weird Ideas That Work*. This valve prevents the water from leaking yet allows drinking without needing to open or close the bottle. The water flows only if pressure is applied, that is, only when the bottle is squeezed. This way, cyclists can drink water with one hand while holding the handlebars with the other and continue pedalling. IDEO (a famous innovation consultancy in Silicon Valley) was commissioned to design a water bottle for *Specialized*, a major bicycle company that also sells helmets, gloves and other accessories for cyclists. How did they go about it? IDEO engineers got the idea of using the valve by looking at heart valves used in heart transplant medicine, something they learned about while working for a medical products company.[41]

When they showed it to *Specialized* executives, it seemed like a new idea because they didn't know about it; it had never been sold in the bicycle industry. Sometimes to surprise a client and look creative you just need to look at other industries and see what artifacts can be used or readapted. Working with companies in industries as diverse as medical instruments, furniture, toys and computers has given IDEO insight into the latest technologies and trained them to "develop quality products quickly and efficiently."[42] In this case, like Play-Doh, a product from one industry was used to create a new product in another.

Technological and scientific revolutions

Technological revolutions result from combining existing things. An example of this is the JAVA software language from Sun Microsystems. One of the creators of JAVA, James Gosling, combined several software languages, including Smalltalk, C++, Cedar/Mesa, and Lisp.[43] In digital technology, Apple's iPod was the 13th MP3 on the market but Apple made only the casing, the industrial design and the interface. Whereas the other parts existed and different suppliers had them on hand: the Toshiba hard drive, the Sony battery, and so on. From concept to market, it took Apple just 8 months. Ray Tomlinson also combined things that already existed to create *email* with the symbol @. On the one hand, this was the code for intra-computer messages, on the other, the transfer protocol for sending files between computers. It didn't take him long, "maybe two or three weeks to put it all together and it worked."[44] The iPod took just 8 months! And email three weeks! That is what is achieved though combination, the secret of creativity.

Bill Gates also combined existing products to create Windows. One of the first jobs Gates did with his partner Paul Allen at Microsoft —says Andrew Hargadon (UC Davies)— was to create the BASIC software language for the Altair computer, a language that allowed others to write software. This language emerged from versions of BASIC (for minicomputers and mainframes) and previous work by Digital Equipment Corporation.[45] Gates acquired the MS-DOS operating system from the small *Seattle Computer Company* for USD 75,000 while the *Word* had already been created in the Xerox PARC (Palo Alto Research Center) laboratory under the name BRAVO, although Xerox never marketed it. Microsoft hired one of Xerox Parc's engineers, Charles Simonyi, who led the team to develop the famous Microsoft Office. Excel is a derivative of Visicalc from Software Arts and Lotus. In short, Gates combined products that already existed, BASIC, the MS-DOS operating system that he bought from another company and Xerox's Word, in addition to the talent of Simonyi and other programmers. This, of course, does not detract from any merit. It is what human creativity is about.

As for Steve Jobs and Apple, note that the first the mouse and the graphics interface did not emerge from this company as many believe, but from the Xerox Parc research laboratory. But Steve Jobs acquired these inventions, improved them and adapted them for the Lisa (1983) and Macintosh (1984) computers. Apple's team of programmers simplified the mouse to a single button and gave it the ability to move documents and other items on screens, as we do today. On the graphics interface, Jobs recalled "being shown a rudimentary graphical user interface. It was incomplete, some of it was not even right, but the germ of the ideas was there. Within ten minutes, it was obvious that every computer would work this way someday."[46] Additionally, Jobs ordered his team to introduce the different fonts (*Times New Roman, Calibri, Arial*, etc.) that he had learned from his calligraphy classes at Reed College.

During that time, Bill Gates and his team at Microsoft made software programs for Apple, with whom they had an exclusivity agreement. But when this agreement expired at the end of 1983, Gates and the Microsoft team were legally free to use Xerox's graphical interface in the operating system that made Microsoft world famous: Windows. When Jobs accused Gates of plagiarism, Gates responded: "Well, Steve, it seems to me that it's like we both had a rich neighbour called Xerox and, when I crept inside his home to steal the television, I found you had already taken it."[47] Jobs liked a quote from Picasso: *good artists copy, great artists steal.*[48]

Henry Ford: the assembly line and cattle slaughterhouses

Another very important technological revolution of our time is the Ford *assembly line* that made mass production of the automobile possible, reducing its price until it became accessible to people of modest means. It was later used to create mass-produced products in other industries. However, it was not invented by Ford. It existed in cow and pig slaughterhouses, from which Ford engineers took the idea and adapted it to car manufacture. In 1906, writer and political activist Upton Sinclair revealed the details of how these slaughterhouses worked, where pigs and cows entered whole at one end and came out cut into parts at the other, while workers worked in their same places as the line advanced. William Klann, head of Ford's engineering department, said, "If they can kill pigs and cows that way, we can build cars that way."[49]

Ford engineers also made use of the concept of having interchangeable parts, which had been known since at least 1801, when Eli Whitney first presented ten identical pistols to the US Congress for the Army. The idea of interchangeable parts allowed all industries to reduce their dependence on craftsmen: if all parts could be made to fit perfectly together, it was no longer necessary to order new parts from craftsmen every time one was missing or no longer useful. It was replaced by another previously designed one in good condition to continue with production. Ford learned about parts interchangeability when he was preparing to build his Model N, the predecessor of the famous Model T. He met Walter Flanders, a machine and tool salesman. Flanders had worked for *Singer Manufacturing Company*, the company that made the famous Singer sewing machines, one of the pioneers in interchangeability.

Few men knew about machines and tools like Flanders. He introduced Ford to Max Wollering, who had worked as a tool inventor for International Harvester and the Hoffman *Hinge and Foundry Company*. Ford hired Wollering as supervisor at the Ford factory in Highland Park (Detroit) and Flanders as production manager. Wollering and Flanders designed the machinery and tools – for drilling, cutting and grinding – which were necessary for engine production. There was nothing new about the interchangeability of parts except for Ford Motor because they had no experience in it.[50]

When Ford adopted these machines and techniques, there were already engineers and mechanics in the automobile industry prepared to use them. The introduction of the first assembly line increased Ford factory productivity by almost 40 percent on the first day and more than 400 percent by the end of the year. Similarly, it initially took workers on the final assembly line just under six hours (350 minutes) to assemble a car; yet a year later, when Ford engineers had perfected the assembly line, this was reduced to an hour and a half (93 minutes).[51]

Modern capitalism had been born and through increased productivity and price reduction it opened the way to mass consumption.

Ford did not invent the car as many say. In 1900 there were 57 companies manufacturing cars in the United States. Of the cars they made 1,681 had steam engines, 1,575 had electric motors, and 936 had gasoline engines. The *internal combustion engine* was then standardized in 1905.[52] The famous Ford Model T is from 1908, the year when 6,000 of them were produced at a price of USD 850. The following year production more than doubled to 14,000 and kept increasing until in 1914 Ford Motor produced 230,000. During this time the price fell from USD 850 to USD 490. As can be seen, Ford's creativity consisted in having combined elements already in existence. That is why Ford concludes: "I invented nothing new. I simply assembled the discoveries of other men behind whom were centuries of work."[53]

The genetic revolution and Einstein's theories

The genetic revolution is also the result of the combination of existing elements. It is powered by a technology called *polymerase chain reaction*, known as PCR, discovered by Kary Mullis in 1983. PCR is to genetics what Ford mass production is to modern day factory, an opportunity for laboratories to mass produce DNA to use first in their experiments and then to develop and produce genetically modified organisms. The critical contribution of PCR as a technology has been to make abundant what was once scarce. But is PCR an "invention" out of nowhere, or a combination? Mullis put together "elements that were already there."[54] He combined existing techniques to make oligonucleotides (particular fragments of DNA) and separate strands from others using gel electrophoresis.

For Albert Einstein, "the combinatorial game" is the essential characteristic of creative thinking, which is not surprising since his ideas were, to some extent, the combination of previous contributions by physicists such as Ernst Mach, Max Planck, Henri Poincaré and Hendrik Lorentz.[55] One way of looking at the combination is *as if it were* an "import and export" business since, strictly speaking, it is about importing ideas or products from one place to export them to another: "importing" silicone and medical valves for artificial hearts to "export them" to the baby bottle and water bottle industry for cyclists; "importing" the cow and pig slaughterhouse line to "export" it to the automobile industry. All great innovations have been born from this ability to combine, from the internet to Tesla's electric car, which combined electricity with engines.

The intersection between art and technology

Creativity not only arises from merging existing things *but from people with different professions*. This is what Frans Johansson argues in his book *The Medici Effect* (2004), a world best-seller several years ago. The name *Medici Effect* is inspired by the 15th century Medici family in Florence (Italy) that financed sculptors, scientists, poets, philosophers, painters and architects. This "intersection of disciplines, professions and cultures" is the combination that allowed for one of the most creative periods in history, the Renaissance, with innovators such as Leonardo Da Vinci and Michelangelo. Diverse teams "can be more creative than homogeneous ones."[56] An example of intersection is the team that designed Apple's Macintosh computer, which according to Jobs, was made up "of musicians, poets, artists, historians, zoologists who were also the best computer scientists in the world."[57] That is, to design Apple's Macintosh, people with different professions and talents came together. People at Apple are able to create products like the iPad because they always try to be at "the intersection of technology and the arts to get the best of both."[58] Facebook is the combination of psychology and sociology with technology.

According to Alan Leshner, CEO of the American Association for the Advancement of Science (AAAS), most major advances involve multiple disciplines.[59] For example, climate change requires the joint work of scientists such as chemists, oceanographers, ecologists and geologists to find solutions. This combination of different disciplines can also be seen in universities, where students combine studies of biology with chemistry, geology with chemistry, mathematics-physics and economics-psychology. That is why in brainstorming meetings held in many companies, people from different disciplines are usually invited to provide different views and perspectives.

The Boston-based consulting firm Bain & Company has consultants specialized in various industries (oil, finance, hospitals, technology companies, etc.) but one of the reasons for their success is that they make their professionals rotate and change areas to learn from other industries. Oriet Gadiesh, one of the top executives, explains that it is proven that "you become better in your area, when you dare to do something different."[60]

The *intersection* that leads to innovation also occurs when people combine different cultures, as did singer Shakira who debuted in the United States with her album *Laundry Service* –a huge success. According to Johansson, Shakira's music is "unusual even in her country of origin, Colombia. Her father is Lebanese and her songs *combined Arabic and Latin sounds in a unique mix* of pop and rock – different from anything Colombian singers had done up to that point. She managed to "take this innovative music and *intersect* it with American tones."[61] Studies show that people who have been raised in different cultures or speak multiple languages exhibit more creativity than those who do not have these skills and life experiences.[62] Buildings and offices have also been designed to encourage intersection. For example, the Manhattan headquarters of Bell Laboratories – where the transistor was invented – had become too small so they decided to move to a new building in New Jersey: the managers knew that creativity could be increased with chance meetings with scientists from different areas. So they designed the hallways to stimulate chance encounters with people with different talents and specialties.

Claude Shannon, an eccentric information theorist, used to ride along Bell's more than two-hundred-meter-long hallways, pedalling a unicycle and juggling three balls, a metaphor for the unstructured environment that had been created in this famous laboratory where, in addition to the transistor, laser technology and cell phones were created. Years later, when Steve Jobs designed the new headquarters for Pixar (the creator of animated films like *Toy Story* and *Finding Nemo*) he became obsessed with the design of the atrium and the place where the toilets would be since they would facilitate personal meetings with people from different areas. He sought to do the same at Apple's new and emblematic headquarters, a circle with an open work space, around a central patio.[63]

Different ways of seeing the same thing

Another aspect of creativity is seeing the same things in new, different ways. Innovators are always trying to reframe their problem -says Sutton- and sometimes the solution is not to invent some technology but, paradoxically, *to eliminate it*, removing it from wherever it may be. For example, for about a century, it was believed that when a submarine sank, there was no safe way to escape. Thousands of sailors died trapped in submarines. In an attempt to solve this drama, a US Navy officer named Charles Momsen invented a device – a life saver with a breathing nose hanging from it – called the Momsen Lung. When someone was trapped in a submarine, they had to put on this device and try to swim to the surface.[64]

However, at the end of the World War, they discovered that almost no one could use the Momsen Lung effectively and began to look into the problem: they realized that if the person was not too deep down, the best they could do was to open the hatch and swim up to the surface, *without using this device*. That is the safest way to escape from a submarine. But as it had been framed as a problem that "needed some technology" thousands of submariners died. This is a case where the answer to the question 'What is the best technology?' is 'No technology!' Swimming to the surface is enough.

Another example is Apple's *iPod shuffle*, which shuffles and selects songs at random, unlike the iPod with a screen. The word shuffle means mixing. This iPod had its screen removed so that the song titles would not be shown. This created a new market for those who wanted to be surprised by the next song to be played, instead of seeing it beforehand on the screen. The designers imagined the surprise experienced by a person driving in their car, not knowing that their favourite song was coming up, different from knowing what is coming as with the *iPod with a screen*. Another example are blackout restaurants (with no lights) where waiters serve with night vision goggles, the kind soldiers use to fight at night. In 1999, an innovator thought that there could be a market for people who wanted to eat in the dark, and with a simple change – by turning off the lights – he created a million-dollar business: the idea of depriving diners of their sight, *intensifying other senses such as taste and smell.*

Furthermore, darkness can give rise to fun situations: *The New York Times* reported that at a blackout restaurant in Beijing, at a table of 30 diners, someone was heard laughing and saying, "I'm touching your head!" while another asked "Who said that?" The first blackout restaurant opened in Zurich but with less frivolous intentions since its goal is to create jobs for the blind and disabled. Totally blind waiters serve Swiss food in total darkness and reservations must be made weeks, sometimes months, in advance.[65]

In these examples there was not, strictly speaking, any creation of a new product but rather of a new market for which a small alteration of the basic elements of the original product was enough. It mainly consisted in *eliminating* technology such as the Momsen Lung in submarines, the screen on the *iPod shuffle* or illumination in restaurants. According to the famous book, *The Little Prince,* "Perfection is achieved not when there is nothing more to add, but when there is *nothing more to remove.*" A lot of creativity can be done by simplifying products and services.

Another example are the so-called "motivational fees" to avoid missing the gym and staying in shape. In general, gyms charge their members a monthly fee regardless of whether they attend or not, and many gyms have more members enrolled than they can actually accommodate since many people pay the fee but do not attend or do so occasionally. Yifan Zhang, a Harvard graduate, noted that this was a sunk cost, especially for people who pay at the beginning of the year.⁶⁶ This motivated her to create *GymPact* in Boston, which basically means that members pay more *if they miss* –a financial penalty for those who lack self-discipline to go to the gym. Members who adhere to this payment method must attend the gym at least 4 times a week and *if they fail to do so, they must pay a fine of $25* for each week they do not comply, or $75 if they leave the gym, except for illness or injury. In this way, a new market was created for people looking to have some *external* incentive not to skip gym.

Routine work and innovative work

Another important aspect to understand creativity -says Sutton- is the difference between *innovative* work and *routine* work. When it comes to routine work, the goal is to eliminate errors and variations. For example, former General Electric CEO Jack Welch was obsessed with *Six Sigma*, the quality control regime. Welch aimed to reduce variations to one error for every million repeated processes. Avoiding variation and errors is critical to success in all industries. Think about the aviation or medical industry: when we board a plane or undergo surgery, we expect everything to go exactly as planned. We don't want there to be any variation since in these cases a variation could be serious. On one occasion, a pilot on Aeroflot line 593 went out of his routine: he wanted to give his 15-year-old son a lesson in mid-flight. He let him handle the plane's control stick and the teenager lost control: they ended up crashing the plane and killing 75 people in 1994.⁶⁷

Another example to distinguish routine work from innovative work are Disney's different divisions. Some Disney employees are in charge of routine work such as running the park which includes organizing people to wait in line, checking ride safety measures, selling tickets, serving food, cleaning the park, etc. It is all routine work and success depends on following the procedures to the letter, repeating them day after day with as little variation as possible. Then there is another division called "Disney Imagineering" – a compounded word from *engineer* and *imagine,* meaning engineers who imagine. They are in charge of inventing new games and attractions for Disney parks.[68]

They are the ones who invented the animated robots in *The Pirates of the Caribbean*, the demon elevator in the *Tower of Terror*, the Aerosmith Rock and Roll roller coaster, etc. This division is expected to try out many different things and have a high error or failure rate until they come up with an innovative product. Those who work in this division – called Disney *imagineers* – tend to be seen as people who often have "bad" ideas, until they invent something great that generates billions of dollars. The point is that creativity and innovative work entail high variation and error rates because only by *increasing the number of attempts* does the chance of creating something innovative increase.

Many attempts to achieve an innovative product

Innovation requires many attempts and perseverance in the face of failure. An example is WD-40 lubricant. It lubricates and protects against moisture and is sold worldwide. The reason they called it WD-40 is because the first 39 formulas failed but the 40th was successful (the name WD-40 stands for Water Displacement-40th Attempt). The work consisted in increasing the variation and with it the failure rate, until the correct formula was discovered. When someone buys a can of WD-40 today they expect to have exactly the same thing, with no variation in each can of WD-40. To achieve this, however, there were many previous failed attempts.

In the 1990s, the consulting firm IDEO had a toy design division called Skyline —now called the *Youth Division*. The job of this division, made up of some six people, was to generate ideas for new toys. When they came up with a good idea, they built a prototype. One of the founders of this division, Brendan Boyle, used to write down all the ideas generated by the group in a spreadsheet. Their 1998 sheet lists, says Sutton, about 4,000 ideas generated for toys, of which 230 became nice prototypes or drawings, 12 were sold but *only 2 or 3 were a commercial success* —an incredibly low success rate or, inversely, a very high error rate. These people keep "failing" all the time to attain a few successes, but you can't have a good idea without having "lots of stupid, bad or crazy ideas."[69]

According to a study of several industries, it takes about 3,000 ideas to arrive at a few successful products.[70] It took James Dyson 15 years and 5,127 prototypes before his *bagless vacuum cleaner* was ready for the market.[71] For Arthur Fry, the inventor of Post-it, innovation is a numbers game: you have to go through 5,000 to 6,000 bad ideas to find one for a successful business, while Thomas Edison repeated that he had not failed but had found "10,000 ways that don't work."[72] In short, creativity involves trying many times and being willing to fail, a very different process from doing routine work. According to these examples, creativity depends on the *number* of attempts such as with the WD-40 lubricant.

In order to turn out some masterpieces, Picasso produced 20,000 artistic works.[73] To publish some articles that revolutionized modern physics, Einstein wrote more than 240 of them. To reach 1039 invention patents, Edison forced himself to create a small invention every 10 days and an important one every 6 months.[74] Dean K. Simonton, author of *Origins of Genius*, has studied geniuses such as Mozart, Shakespeare, Picasso, Einstein and Darwin and concludes that their genius comes from the great *number* and *variety* of ideas and works they produced. The best predictor of whether someone will receive an award for their creativity, such as the Nobel Prize, is the number of scientific papers they have published.[75] Genius and innovations are therefore the result of effort and perseverance.

Failure does not exist

In Silicon Valley there is a philosophy that failure in business – and especially if it is to innovate – is not a problem because success generally requires several attempts. There are few who succeed on their first attempt. According to Jobs, the penalty for trying to start a company in Silicon Valley "does not exist."[76] It is one of the few places in the world where having failed in a business is an "honour" since it means that at least one has tried. In fact, there are investment funds that refuse to lend to those who have not failed because they understand that failing builds character and provides experience for the next attempt. Studies show that entrepreneurs who have failed are 20% more likely to succeed on their next attempt than those who are first timers.[77]

On the other hand, in other parts of the world (e.g. Europe and Japan) failure is harshly penalized. German law for example does not allow anyone who has filed for bankruptcy to become a company CEO. The opposite is true in Israel, with one of the most lenient bankruptcy laws. It is one of the easiest countries to start a business after failing in another. This contrast between incentives in different places or countries is decisive when it comes to promoting innovation.

Some companies offer incentives to innovate but this is not generally the rule. Professors Gina O'Connor and Christopher M. McDermott did a study of ten companies over a six-year period and found that the lack of innovation was due to the wrong incentives: strong *penalties* for employees who failed, rather than offering strong *rewards* for doing something creative.[78] Employees with good ideas often prefer not to ask their company bosses to allocate resources to research or manufacture a prototype, for fear of being fired or sanctioned if they are not successful. In companies with this philosophy, innovation is almost impossible. A *high tolerance for failure* is an essential trait for a company that aims to innovate.

The creative process

The brain is an "intelligent memory" that records absolutely everything that happens to us in life, what we read, see or is told to us, storing it in what some scientists call "mental drawers."[79] According to studies, the best ideas arise when we are relaxed, as in this state the drawers *combine* the stored information more easily. Many times ideas arise in places like the shower or the beach. On the other hand, when the brain is focused on a specific task or stressed about finishing something, the ability to combine decreases significantly. A study by Teresa Amabile (Harvard) of 177 employees and 7 companies found that people are *less creative* when under pressure.[80]

For this reason, many companies give their employees relaxed spaces (rooms with table-tennis or soccer tables) to facilitate creativity. At Corning, for example, over a decade ago the head of the research group, Lina Echeverría, created a "creativity room" where employees could talk about anything in order to facilitate the combination of ideas or things.[81] Corning is a company with 150 years of history: it made glass for Edison's light bulbs and *Pyrex* glass pans that can be taken out of the freezer and heated directly in the oven without breaking, among other innovative products.

Since creativity works better when individuals are relaxed than when under stress or nervous tension, the worst enemy is criticism. One's own or from others. It creates tension and conditions people. When you set out to generate ideas, it is best to stop all *criticism and judgment activities*, which is difficult to do given that school, parents and society push us to constantly judge what is good or bad. For creativity, criticism and judgment are negative, they act as inhibitors. When you reach an obstacle or blockage (an *impasse*) it is advisable not to insist on the issue but to let it rest, to do something different for a few hours or even days. During that time the brain keeps thinking in a process called the *incubation period* until, at a given moment, the subconscious mind sends up a solution or shows a more effective way to approach the problem.

This is not a book about creativity techniques, though a few are worth mentioning. The most common is *brainstorming*, meetings held to *storm out ideas*. Expert advice for having a good brainstorming session is to "argue as if you were right but to listen as if you were wrong" and not criticize when ideas are being generated, because, as we have said, that would inhibit creativity, your own and your colleagues'. There is also the Scamper technique whose spelling means *Substitute, combine, adapt, modify, put to another use, eliminate* and *rearrange*. It is a mnemonic to remember various alternatives. For example, if a team leader wants to create an environment where there is more collaboration, they may *substitute* the person on their team who acts selfishly or directly *remove* them from the team.

Creativity is not only a requirement in the competitive global job market but in life in general. Studies show that everyone needs creativity in their lives, from a housewife who manages to feed three children with just two eggs by turning them into an omelette with leftovers from the previous day, to an employee of a charitable foundation who must figure out how to convince others to donate money. A study by Mark Beeman (Northwestern University) found that 40% of the time, people solve problems logically, but in the other 60% they do so through creative *insight*, experienced at unusual times or places like the shower or while listening to music in the car.[82]

In conclusion, creativity is the combination of pre-existing elements to turn into new syntheses. As art historian E. H. Gombrich says, people do not "have sudden ideas, they construct them and *combine* them with what they already know."[83] The English expression 'Thinking outside the box' is synonymous with being creative. But strictly speaking it is inaccurate because the examples we have seen show us that when someone thinks "outside their box" they do not do so in a *vacuum* but in *other boxes*, in other industries from where they extract ideas and materials to combine. In 1910, Ford engineers seemed to be thinking outside their boxes, but strictly speaking, they were just doing it "in different boxes" (the cow and pig slaughterhouses).[84]

And it could not be any other way, since to create something, humans always start from some matter: they cannot create something from nothing, as does God or some superior entity. For a laboratory to generate a living being (person or animal) it needs the genetic matter of another and techniques such as *in vitro* fertilization, cloning, etc. Human beings cannot create oxygen from nothing. NASA wants to take oxygen to Mars to make it habitable and is building a device to produce it there, the *Mars Oxigen In Situ Experiment* (Moxie). But to achieve this the device must combine with the carbon dioxide that exists on Mars.[85] Theology uses the expression creation *from matter* for human creation *(creatio ex materia)* and creation *from nothing* to refer to God's creation *(creatio ex nihilo)*. Much of a team's work that aims to innovate is therefore to seek combinations of ideas, materials, products, disciplines or cultures, just like the pilot who combined suitcases with wheels or the musicians, historians, zoologists and computer engineers who created the Apple Macintosh.

> If you can increase the number of experiments, you can increase the number of innovations.[86]
>
> **Jeff Bezos**

Chapter 3

Entrepreneurial capitalism and the skills of innovators

The *entrepreneurs* are the main protagonists of innovation today. They set up companies against all odds, often with little capital. Many of these entrepreneurs invent technologies or products that revolutionise people's lives. Entrepreneurship is a management and leadership style that involves pursuing business opportunities, *regardless of the resources available*, according to the definition of Harvard professor Howard H. Stevenson. We sometimes forget that it is people like Bill Gates who, in 1978 at the age of 18, started off with a small group of programmers, or Steve Jobs who initiated Apple in the *garage* of his parents' house. In 1976 he sold his Volkswagen and Wozniak his Hewlett Packard calculator, raising $1,300 to start Apple.[87] Bezos started Amazon in 1994 with $50,000 from his savings and later his parents put in $250,000 more.

Why is there so much talk about entrepreneurs today? Firstly, due to the resurgence of *entrepreneurial capitalism*. Until the late 1970s, small businesses were not thought to ever play an important role because, among other reasons, they were less efficient than large businesses. It was even believed that there would come a day with global predominance of multinational companies. Economist John Kenneth Galbraith spread his theory of "countervailing powers" according to which the power of large companies should be compensated by "large unions" and "large states." However, recent decades have seen the opposite taking place. Small businesses in America produced 20% of manufactured goods sold in 1976, but by 1986 the figure had increased to more than 25%.[88] Steven Rogers, business profesor, points out: "In the 1960s, 1 out of every 4 persons in the United States worked for a Fortune 500 company. Today, only 1 out of every 14 people works for these companies. Employment at Fortune 500 companies peaked at 16.5 million people in 1979 and has steadily declined every year to approximately 10.5 million people today."[89]

Something similar happened in Europe. Employment in small industries also increased: in the Netherlands total industrial employment grew from 68.3% in 1978 to 71.8% in 1986; in the United Kingdom it grew from 30.7% in 1979 to 39.9% in 1986, and in Germany from 54.8% in 1970 to 57.9% in 1987, and similarly in other European countries. This has created a new "model" of capitalism that researchers call "entrepreneurial" replacing the "managerial" model of large companies. Many of the most innovative entrepreneurs of our time come from the United States, the country of *entrepreneurial capitalism*: Steve Jobs, Bill Gates, Jeff Bezos, Mark Zuckerbeg, Elon Musk, etc. One in ten adults in the United States started or managed a business between 1999 and 2011.[90]

Secondly, the media exalts entrepreneurs who innovate for their unique characteristics: their great *perseverance*, their *knowledge, vision* and especially because they are a *threat* to large companies since they sometimes create innovative technologies and products. Such is the case of Apple's personal computer that competed with IBM in the 1970s and 1980s when Apple was a small company, or of Amazon, that dethroned large publishers and shopping malls in terms of sales. These are the new modern heroes, media characters often involved in fights (especially when starting) in the style of "little David against giant Goliath." When Amazon and Apple started, they competed against larger companies before becoming large themselves.

Schumpeter warned of the existence of "creative destruction" as new technologies destroy large companies while creating new ones, revolutionizing the structure of the economy. In the early 20th century, the automobile replaced horse carts and in the mid-1970s the personal computer replaced the typewriter. Now this destruction is even more intense: the average life of a large company in the Standard & Poors 500 has been reduced from 35 years in 1975 to an average of less than 20 years today. Of the 25 technological companies that were at the top of the ranking 30 years ago, only a few remain today (less than 4) that are still leaders.[91]

Knowledge, vision and capital for entrepreneurs

The *knowledge* that many entrepreneurs possess is the most important factor when it comes to innovating, rather than natural resources. At the beginning of the 20th century, Rockefeller, the richest man in the world, became rich with oil (Standard Oil) but today the richest, Bezos or Gates, have become wealthy based on knowledge. Analysts estimate the intellectual property market is $100 billion a year. At IBM, patents and licenses represent about 15% of its profits.[92]

According to consulting firm Ocean Tomo (experts on intellectual property), in 2020 patents and software programs, marketing and highly trained employees (intangible assets) represented approximately 90% of the assets of companies such as Microsoft, Intel or Amgen, whereas in 1975 they barely reached 17%. The companies analyzed in this study are the 500 that make up the Standard & Poors 500 stock index in the United States, and intangible assets are calculated by subtracting the value of the tangible assets from the market capitalization.[93]

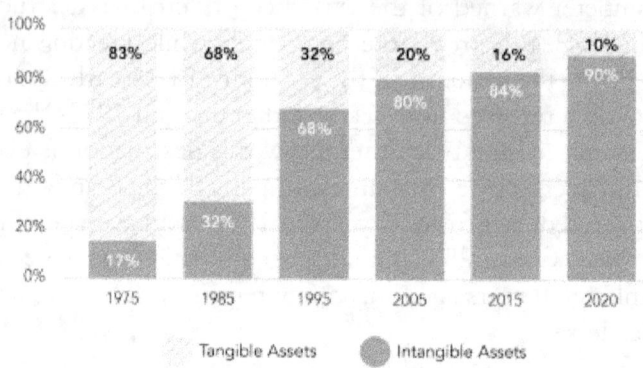

What about Europe? Analyzing the *S&P Europe* 350 index, which comprises 350 leading companies from 16 developed European market countries, the result is that Europe continues to be the second economy –behind the United States– in the amount of intangible assets, still far ahead of the main Asian markets.

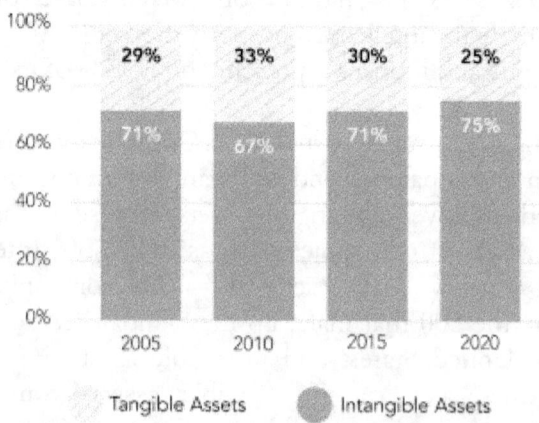

Source: Ocean Tomo LLc (www.oceantomo.com).

92% of the technology entrepreneurs surveyed by the Kauffman Foundation have a university degree, 31% have a master's degree and 10% have a doctorate.[94] Robert Noyce (Intel), the inventor of the chip, was an M.I.T doctor in physics; Larry Page (Google) has a master's degree in computer science from Stanford; Jeff Bezos (Amazon) is an electrical and computer engineer from Princeton and Mark Zuckerberg (Facebook) studied psychology and computing at Harvard. What about Steve Jobs? He never earned a college degree, but his partner, Wozniak, was a computer engineer and Jobs surrounded himself with many talented programmers such as Bill Atkinson. Just because a great idea appears at a moment of relaxation or *alpha* or *gamma* waves –as creativity scholars say– it does not mean that knowledge and a good education have not been necessary.

Knowledge is the "price of a ticket to the game of creativity."[95] How can someone hope to revolutionise the computing industry if they don't know a great deal about software? Knowledge is – along with economic freedom – the key to the economic prosperity of nations. Einstein prophesied,

> In the future, only *people who understand how to generate knowledge* and how to protect it will be successful (...) The other nations will be left with their beautiful coastlines, their churches, their mines... but they will probably not have the same flags or the same borders. And much less economic power.[96]

These entrepreneurs are also fascinating because of their *vision*. A vision is an informed, long-term look at the destiny of a company and the industry. When Bill Gates started programming in the 1970s, computer enthusiasts traded and bought *hardware*, the hard parts of the computer. Gates remembers,

> There was no such thing as a software industry. We had the insight that you could create one. And we did. That was the most important idea that I ever had.[97]

Mark Zuckerberg, the son of a dentist, rejected an $800 million offer from Viacom (MTV) to sell Facebook in 2005 and a $1 billion offer from Yahoo in 2006 to accomplish his vision of creating a global network of people and friends with Facebook. In 2004, when he had just started Facebook and was only 20 years old, he turned down a $10 million offer from a Manhattan investor to go to California. With two friends, no car, no money and no financial connections he set out to expand Facebook. Zuckerberg wanted to change the world, something different from the popular dream of becoming a millionaire. Zuckerberg: "I don't really need the money. Besides, I don't think I'll ever have such a good idea again."[98]

Where do entrepreneurs get their capital from? Approximately 75% of startups are initiated with their own funds, from the entrepreneurs' friends or family (bootstrapped, self-financed). Sums of 10,000 to 1 million dollars are obtained from the so-called "angels" (individual investors).[99] For example, Mike Markkula was Apple's angel investor when this company had only 8 employees and operated in the *garage* of Steve Jobs' parents' house. Markkula invested $91,000 in cash and opened a line of credit for $250,000. Angels invest in more than 50,000 startups a year in the United States.

Venture capital funds finance from 1 to 20 million dollars. The companies financed by these funds today make up almost 20% of the United States GDP.[100] Amazon raised 8 million from these funds and 54 million from the public offering of shares in 1997. These funds receive around 2,000 business plans a year asking for money and they invest in more than 5,000 startups a year in the United States. Large corporations invest $5 million to $50 million in startups: Intel has invested in 1,100 startups –a total of $7.9 billion– to boost demand for its chips.

Another source is *crowdsourcing* such as AngelList or Kickstarter, online sites where entrepreneurs post their inventions or projects and where investors look for opportunities. AngelList went up from 1,500 companies in 2010 to 38,000 in 2012. Kickstarter grew from $28 million in 2010 to $320 million in 2012. Many entrepreneurs in Latin America often go to Silicon Valley to raise capital. For example, Venezuelan Andrés Moreno, founder of *Open English*, an English online learning site, realised early on that raising funds in Latin America was very challenging, because there was "not a great venture capital culture there."[101] Moreno managed to raise 120 million dollars in *venture capital* but to do so he had to emigrate. Latin America lacks venture capital: in 2020 it was barely $4 billion while in the United States it was $130 billion, according to some studies.[102]

The creative skills of innovators

The big question that many entrepreneurs ask themselves, especially young people who dream of being the next Steve Jobs or Elon Musk (Tesla) is: How do these innovation titans find ideas and business opportunities? A few years ago professors from Harvard, M.I.T and Pennsylvania universities set out to study this. They interviewed and evaluated about 80 innovators and 400 executives, including Jeff Bezos, Steve Jobs, Pierre Omidyar and Howard Schultz. Their idea was to ask them: How did you come up with your great idea? How did you find your big opportunity? Do you have any particular skills that help you come up with good ideas? These professors (Jeffrey H. Dyer, Hal B. Gregersen and Clayton Christensen) published their study in 2008 ("Entrepreuners Behaviors, Opportunity Recognition, and the Origins of Innovative Ventures") and also a book, *The Innovator's DNA* (2011).

The first thing they discovered is that people like Jobs or Bezos are good at *associative thinking*, also called *lateral thinking*, which consists in combining things or ideas whose combination does not seem reasonable at first glance. An example is the connection that Jobs made between calligraphy and computing, which today allows us to choose different fonts when writing on our computers such as Times New Roman, Courier, Arial, etc. Jobs recalled,

Reed College at that time offered perhaps the best calligraphy instruction in the country. Throughout the campus every poster, every label on every drawer, was beautifully hand calligraphed. Because I had dropped out and didn't have to take the normal classes, I decided to take a calligraphy class to learn how to do this. I learned about serif and san serif typefaces, about varying the amount of space between different letter combinations, about what makes great typography great. It was beautiful, historical. artistically subtle in a way that science can't capture, and I found it fascinating. None of this had even a hope of any practical application in my life. But 10 years later, when we were designing the first Macintosh computer, it all came back to me. And we designed it all into the Mac. It was the first computer with beautiful typography. If I had never dropped in on that single course in college, the Mac would have never had multiple typefaces or proportionally spaced fonts. And since Windows just copied the Mac, it's likely that no personal computer would have them.[103]

That's why Jobs states that creativity is "connecting things. When you ask creative people how they did something, they feel a little guilty because they didn't really do it, they just *saw something*…"[104] Another example is Niklas Zennstrom, inventor of Skype, who advises spending time "seeing and combining certain things (...) and understanding how seemingly unrelated things could have something to do with each other."[105] As can be seen, we return to the notion of combination, the basis of creativity.

The study found that innovators put into action certain behaviors called *creative skills* that differ from *delivery skills*.[106] The delivery ones are analyzing, planning, implementing in detail, and self-discipline to work long hours. These are the skills that many company executives and employees have. On the other hand, *creative skills* are questioning, observing, experimenting and networking (explained below). According to the study, innovators spend *50% more of their time* questioning, observing, experimenting and *networking* than executives who have not done any innovation. This means almost *one more day per week* than those who only use delivery skills.[107] Why is it that they do these four things more often than others?

The answer is that "they have the courage to innovate."[108] They also found that *creative skills* are significantly correlated with starting innovative businesses and that they are correlated with each other, suggesting that a person who puts into action some of these creative skills – for example, observing – is also likely to put other skills into action such as *questioning* or *experimenting*.

Finally, the study found that these innovators want to *change the world*. Zennstrom (Skype): "'I thrive on changing the *status quo*; that's what motivates me. I definitely want to change the world."[109] Steve Jobs: "I want to put a ding in the universe" and "we are here to make a dent in the universe. Otherwise, why even be here?"[110] There are a lot of studies that say that most people prefer the current state of things (it's called the *status quo* bias). On the other hand, innovators have an *anti-status quo* bias, a passion for going against what is established or known. Below, I discuss examples of these creative skills: questioning, observing, experimenting and networking. I quote the words of famous innovators because they accurately describe their way of reasoning.

Questioning

Einstein and a great many philosophers maintain that the important thing is to ask the right question and not to stop questioning. Einstein: "If I only had the right question…"[111] Well, Jobs asked himself: "Why isn't there a middle category of device in between a laptop and a smart phone? and "What if we build one?"[112] The *iPad* emerged from these questions. Another case is that of Ratan Tata, from the Tata group (India). For him, you have to "question the unquestionable" and he did so when he saw an Indian family (father, mother and son), on a motorcycle getting wet in the rain[113].

Tata wondered: "Why can't this family own a car and avoid the rain?"[114] His passion for solving this problem motivated him to build the cheapest car in the world, the NANO (for $2,000 in 2009). Another example in the study is that of Marc Benioff, founder of *Salesforce*, which today sells software over the internet – cloud services – with sales of 6.2 billion dollars in 2016. Benioff says he was swimming with dolphins in Hawaii and asked himself: "Why aren't all enterprise software applications built like Amazon and eBay? Why are we still loading and upgrading software the way that we have doing all this time when we have the Internet? And that was a fundamental breakthrough for me. And that´s the genesis of *Salesforce*…"[115]

We must keep in mind that *asking* and *questioning* are not so common among adults though they are among children. Many are afraid to question the *status quo*, what is established or blessed by society. It is the fear of going against what the majority thinks, as if it possessed the truth. Philosopher Ortega y Gasset explains it: "Is the decision of eight individuals adopted against that of two? A serious mistake! The eight will probably include more fools than the two."[116] This fear can be seen at the end of conferences or work meetings when the speaker or boss asks: "Any questions?" And no one wants to ask for fear of showing they have not understood. This inhibition begins in primary school: we don't want to be seen as stupid by our classmates or teachers, so it is safer to stay silent.

Google's former head of innovation, Frederik Pferdt, highlights the difference between the number of questions we ask as children and those as adults and comments that his oldest son probably asks "some 180 questions a day. But as adults, maybe we just ask 2 to 4 questions a day."[117] Warren Berger comments that the question that led to the invention of the Polaroid instant camera came from the founder of Polaroid's four-year-old daughter who asked, "Dad, why do we have to wait for the picture?"[118]. Pierre Omidyar (eBay): "I often preface my questions by saying 'I like to be the guy that asks a lot of dumb questions about why things are the way they are'." That way he relaxes the tension in the environment so that questions arise.[119] This is essential for something we will see later, "psychological safety", which is the ideal attitude to create a relaxed environment where people feel comfortable being themselves and questioning what is taken for granted or known.

Observing

Innovators' second skill is simple *observation*, although it is combined with questioning. Through observation, Starbucks founder

LA INNOVACION EN SILICON VALEY

Howard Schultz discovered *latte* coffee, later one of the company's most successful products. During a trip to Milan to attend an international household goods fair, Schultz decided to walk to the fair, some 15 minutes from his hotel. That was when he discovered *espresso* bars. He went into one to look around and had an *espresso*. Later he passed by another one and noticed that the man behind the counter greeted each customer by their name. The man and the customers were laughing, talking and enjoying the moment. Schultz says these bars offered comfort and a sense of extended family. He continued walking through the streets of Milan to look at more *espresso* bars and suddenly had a revelation:

> Starbucks sold great coffee beans, but we didn't serve coffee by the cup. If we could recreate in America the authentic Italian coffee bar culture, it might resonate with other Americans the way it did with me. Starbucks could be a great experience, and not just a great retail store. I stayed in Milan about a week. I continued my walks through the city, getting lost every day. One morning I took a train ride to Verona. Its coffee bars were much like Milan's, and in one, I mimicked someone and ordered a caffe *latte*, my first taste of that drink . . . Of all the coffee experts I had met, none had ever mentioned this drink. No one in America knows about this, I thought. *I've got to take it back with me.*'[120]

The study states that those who live at least 3 months in a foreign country are 35% more likely to start a new venture or invent an innovative product.[121] When traveling or living abroad they observe other customs and inventions they can then take back to their country and combine them with some other innovation, as Schultz did. Another example of observation is made by Jeff Bezos, founder of Amazon, when he was working at another company in 1994. One day he was reading on a site which said the Internet was growing at 2,300 percent per year. Bezos remembers,

It was a wake-up call. You have to keep in mind that human beings are not very good at understanding exponential growth. It is not something we see in our everyday life.[122]

Scott Cook is the founder of Intuit, the company that makes small business accounting and tax software, widely used by family business owners in the United States. Cook combined software with accounting and this came from observing the problems that his wife had. She was an accountant and complained about wasting time and how complicated it was to keep accounts for her clients. It was this "observation combined with an understanding of what computers could do well and not do well started Intuit."[123] Many products of this company arise from seeing how customers deal with practical problems. Cook remembers that a friend who worked for Apple had shown him the applications of the LISA computer before it went on sale. He was so excited about these applications that he left the Apple headquarters, drove to the nearest restaurant and sat down with a writing pad to note down the ideas he had observed.

According to Tom Kelley (IDEO), the role of the anthropologist is "the best source of innovation at IDEO" because anthropologists have developed techniques to observe human beings in their natural habitat and learn from their behaviors.[124] When Procter & Gamble (P&G) asked IDEO to design new toothbrushes for children, the IDEO team responded that they first needed to observe children brushing their teeth. P&G executives thought this was an odd request. "Don't they know how children brush their teeth?" But IDEO designers needed to see how kids held their brushes and didn't want to make assumptions. They discovered that children do not have the motor skills of adults to manipulate brushes. So they thought: "What happens if we make children's toothbrushes bigger?" The way they hold the brush is totally different from that of adults. Adults have greater dexterity in their hands and tend to use their fingers to manipulate the toothbrush, while children grip the brush with the palm of their hand, making a fist. After observing the way children did this, IDEO designed the Oral-B Kids brush that became a global bestseller.[125]

Experimenting

Of all the creative skills, the study found that experimentation is the skill that most distinguishes innovators. Gordon Moore, co-founder of Intel, explains that most of what he learned was "by trial and error" and Bezos claims that experiments are key to innovation because "they rarely turn out the way as you expect, and you learn so much."[126] At Amazon, employees are allowed to experiment. They have a process called *working backwards*. What they do is allow any employee to write a six-page document. The document begins with a press release that announces a new product or service and explains the reasons why it is great. It includes some frequently asked questions and usually a prototype. They then present it to their bosses to see if anyone is willing to invest resources to develop it.

Let us remember that at the beginning Bezos saw that the Internet was the ideal vehicle to offer an online books catalog. That is why when he launched Amazon.com, he called it "Earth´s Biggest Bookstore." Amazon offered the largest selection of books without having made any investment in stores, warehouses, or inventory (wholesale Ingram stored and shipped the books). But Bezos had bigger dreams than simply selling books. Even before Amazon was profitable, he saw an opportunity for the company to sell other products, from television sets to toys. So he made a very risky bet. He decided to build a series of 850,000-square-foot warehouses across the country. Originally, they operated at 10 percent capacity. Today Amazon is positioned as the leader in online sales, with multiple product lines.[127]

In 2007, Amazon launched the Kindle tablet, which captured 90 percent of the market. Today it rents data storage and computing power through cloud services, competing with computer giants like IBM. According to some studies, 25 percent of small and medium-sized businesses in Silicon Valley use Amazon cloud services. In 2019, Bezos announced his intention to build floating cities in space in the shape of cylinders that rotate and replicate the Earth's gravity in order to put a billion people to live there, with a climate like that of Maui (Hawaii), with no earthquakes or rain. With each passing year he becomes more convinced that his company *Blue Origin* (a spaceship builder) is his most important work.[128]

According to Bezos, humans consume, on average, 11,000 watts and going up. To deal with it, he recommends covering the Earth's surface with solar panels. In his vision, humans will need more energy, which is abundant in space, and billions of people could live there. Besides, if there were that many people, "we would have a thousand Einsteins and a thousand Mozarts and unlimited solar energy: that is the world I want my great-great-grandchildren's great-grandchildren to live in." As we can see, the largest *online* bookstore on Earth –his original idea– has changed several times thanks to its ability to experiment with different business models. Where does his proneness to experiment come from?

Some of it comes from his genetics. When he was tired of sleeping in his crib he tried to take it apart with a screwdriver. But another part comes from his family environment, with modest resources. When he was 12, he desperately wanted a new device called the *Infinity Cube*, a set of mirrors that reflected each other. He was fascinated by this toy; it was very expensive so he bought some mirrors and other parts and built his own version of the *Infinity Cube*. It was the summers at his grandfather's ranch where he spent time doing experiments that increased his creative capacity. Bezos notes,

> I really gained confidence in my creative ability by helping my grandfather fix things on his ranch. He often didn't have the money to fix things, so we had to improvise.[129]

Another example of *experimentation* is that of Michael Dell. How did he discover the "Dell business model"? By taking apart the computers that his parents struggled to buy him. In 1980 he was looking forward to his sixteenth birthday. He went with his father to pick up the Apple II computer that had arrived by UPS; when they got home, he jumped out of the car and the first thing he did was disassemble the computer. Dell recalled: "My parents were infuriated. An Apple cost a lot of money in those days... But I wanted to look inside and see how it worked."[130]

Dell's desire to understand how an Apple II worked led to several experiments. He purchased a variety of components to improve his personal computer, such as memory, hard drives, faster modens, and larger monitors. At that time, the IBM PC sold for $2,500 - $3,000. But the components could be purchased separately for only $600 or $700. Dell asked, "Why does it cost five times more to buy a PC in the store than the parts cost?"[131] He realised that he could buy the components separately and assemble them according to what each client wanted for less than the price of a complete computer. That is how the "Dell direct" business model was born.

Another case of *experimentation* is that of Jennifer Hyman, the founder of *Rent The Runaway*. Hyman decided to test whether women would rent designer dresses online. At Harvard Business School – where she studied – she set up a stand before a student event to see if girls would rent designer dresses. She got some dresses on loan and got a very positive response. But she wondered, "Well, what if they weren't able to try on the dresses?"[132] She then did an experiment in New York City targeting about a thousand women. She created a very rudimentary website with some photos of the dresses to see if women would rent them without trying them on. From the experiment she learnt that they even rented online and often ordered two sizes to ensure the correct size. Some six years later, at the inauguration of Barack Obama's second presidential term in the White House, 85% of the women wore a dress rented through *Rent The Runway*.

Hyman's experiments recall one of the most useful pieces of advice given by innovation experts: create a place in the company where it is safe to fail, a place to experiment and learn without doing harm in terms of time or money. Medical students practice on corpses and that way they learn without causing harm. A former director of IDEO, Diego Rodriguez, asks in this regard, "Where is your place for failing?"

There are several ways to experiment and learn without incurring large costs.

One of them is setting up a rudimentary website to put the product to the test like Hyman did, and see if it has acceptance among customers or investors. The creators of Dropbox, the cloud storage site, put their product on a hacker page called *Hacker News*, to test things. In this way they obtained feedback from end users, which allowed them to learn and improve their product before launching it on the market. It is therefore essential to ask if there is a place to fail in the company, a place to try things out and for the team to learn, before jumping into the void or spending a large amount of money on something that has not yet been proven to work.

Networking

Finally we have this last skill: *networking*, which is basically using the knowledge or technologies of others to use them in your own venture. This is possible when you have an interesting network of people with knowledge and different ways of thinking. Steve Jobs used his network to found Pixar. Alan Kay, inventor of the Xerox Alto computer, told Jobs, "Go visit these crazy guys in San Rafael, California."[133] The "crazy guys" were Ed Catmull and Alvy Ray who, from a small company, *Industrial Light & Magic*, made special effects for George Lucas, the creator of *Star Wars*. Jobs bought this small company for a few million dollars and renamed it Pixar, and that technology was used to make the *Toy Story, Ratatouille, Inside Out* and *Coco* movies, among other hits. Jobs did not invent the technology that these "crazy people" developed. But he used his network to build a fabulous company that is worth billions of dollars today.

Networking comes from relating to people outside one's area of expertise, as seen with the idea of *intersection* and the *Medici effect*. Pierre Omidyar, (eBay) says he looks for information from unexpected places and from people who are not experts. Many of his new ideas come from unusual places. Omidyar remarked,

The cliché would be, rather than talking to the CEO, I would want to talk to someone in the mailroom, something like that. I really look for people that have diverse backgrounds, diverse ways of thinking about things; what I try to do is just be exposed to some different styles of thinking.[134]

Sociologist Ron Burt (University of Chicago) studied 673 managers of technology companies in the United States and found that those with the most contacts in their network generated the most valuable ideas. According to Burt,

> People connected to groups beyond their own can expect to find themselves delivering valuable ideas, seeming to be gifted with creativity. This is not creativity born of genius; it is creativity as an import-export business. An idea mundane in one group can be a valuable insight in another.[135]

Such is the case of the compound that was used in charcoal heating and later used to make plasticine (Play-Doh), or the *medical valves* to make spouts for cyclists' bottles. The Procter & Gamble (P&G) teams have a network made up of independent researchers, companies and sometimes competitors. For example, NineSigma and InnoCentive help P&G prepare technology reports that describe problems that P&G is trying to solve. P&G distributes them to thousands of researchers around the world. This has helped P&G's source of external ideas go up from 10% in 2000 to 45% in 2006.[136]

P&G uses this network of contacts to come up with its own innovations. They also send their employees to learn from other companies. They once sent HR and Marketing staff to Google for four to six weeks to observe how they did things and see if there were ideas they could copy or learn from them. A P&G employee said they learned interesting things about digital marketing at Google, specifically how to identify mother blogs or "mom bloggers" – those that recommend or review products and influence other consumers –

in order to give them instructions every time that P&G launched a new product for mothers.

Another modality that could be considered *networking* – although it does not appear in the study – is buying companies that have discovered innovative technologies or products. Economist Willard Mueller studied DuPont chemicals to see where they had come from. He analised the top 25 product and process innovations that had taken place between 1920 and 1950, which together accounted for 45 percent of DuPont's total sales in 1948. Of the 25 products, DuPont had developed only 10 internally and acquired the rest.[137] DuPont's research and development laboratories are in charge of research but also act as doors between the company's needs and technologies that come up in other places or companies that are part of its network. Many technology companies such as Cisco, Google, Microsoft, etc. buy start-ups to fill some gap they may have in some knowledge. In 2011 Google acquired more than 100 companies, many of them start-ups.[138]

Practicing creative skills

When hearing about these skills, some may think, "But if I am not creative, what can I do?" The good news is that these skills can be practiced and some people have done so. In a pharmaceutical company, an executive began to practice questioning techniques every day to identify strategic points in his division. "I just improved my ability to question," says this executive. After just 3 months, his boss told him that he had become the most effective thinker and promoted him to a strategic planning position. Creativity experts say that individuals and teams can increase their creativity through practice. According to brothers David and Tom Kelley (IDEO), creativity is like a "muscle that can be strengthened and nurtured through effort and experience."[139] Creativity can be improved by practicing *creative skills* in the same way that people practice *delivery skills* in their jobs. How can one practice them? The book *The Innovator's DNA* offers some tips and advice.

For *questioning* skills, they advise asking questions that impose constraints or remove constraints such as "What would happen if we lost our biggest customer?" or "What would you do *if money were no object?*"[140] This last question was asked by Steve Jobs because he believed that to achieve excellence you did not have to think about money limitations. According to Marissa Mayer (former vicepresident of search products at Google), creativity loves constraint. Some people think that artistic work is like an uncontrolled or unguided effort. However, "some of the most inspiring art forms (haikus, sonatas, religious paintings) are fraught with constraints. They are beautiful because creativity triumphed over rules…Creativity, in fact, thrives best when constrained."[141]

When there are some restrictions, studies show that there is more creativity than when there is none.[142] Studies have found that many problems are poorly defined, that some of the building blocks are incomplete or the search space is extremely large. It is like asking a group of people to invent a sport *without any rules*. It would be too big a "space" and it would end up being a non-sport, something difficult or impossible to play because, for it to be a sport, it must have some rules.

To *observe*, the authors of *The Innovator's DNA* advise looking at what a people (customers) do in real-life situations: see what they like and what they do not. Think of something that can *make their life easier*. Ask yourself, What job are they trying to do? What could I invent to make it easier for them?

To *experiment*, they advise learning a new skill or trade, building prototypes of ideas or disassembling products to learn something. For instance, a computer or a cell phone. As to networking, they advise having dinner or lunch with a person from a different profession or job – once a week – or attending a conference on a topic you know nothing about. Below is a survey developed by professors Dyer, Gregersen and Christensen to distinguish the innovative entrepreneurs from executives.[143]

Questioning

1. I am always asking questions.

2. I am constantly asking questions to get at the root of the problem.

3. Others are frustrated by the frequency of my questions.
4. I often ask questions that challenge the *status quo*.

5. I regularly ask questions that challenge others' fundamental assumptions.

6. I am constantly asking questions to understand why products and projects underperform

Observing

1. New business ideas often come to me when directly observing how people interact with products and services.

2. I have a continuous flow of new business ideas that comes through observing the world.

3. I regularly observe customers' use of our company's products and services to get new ideas.

4. By paying attention to everyday experiences, I often get new business ideas.

Experimenting

1. I love to experiment to understand how things work and to create new ways of doing things.

2. I frequently experiment to create new ways of doing things.

3. I am adventurous, always looking for new experiences.

4. I actively search for new ideas through experimenting.

5. I have a history of taking things apart.

Networking

1. I have a network of individuals whom I trust to bring a new perspective and refine new ideas.

2. I attend many diverse professional and/or academic conferences outside of my industry/profession.

3. I initiate meetings with people outside of my industry to spark ideas for a new product, service, or customer base.

4. I have a large network of contacts with whom I frequently interact to get ideas for new products, services, and customers.

Some measures to promote a culture of innovation

These famous innovators (Jobs, Gates, Dell, Bezos, Musk, Omidyar, etc.) realised that it is impossible to participate in every work team in their company and that interaction with most of their employees would be limited and occasional. Therefore, they took care to instill commitment to innovation throughout their organization. To do this, they implemented practices that help create a culture or an environment *favourable to innovation* and take on people with creative potential. For example, Google developed a 21-question questionnaire to select candidates (Google Labs Aptitude Test). One of the questions is "How many different ways can you color an icosahedron…?" Others are designed to test whether the candidate makes a creative effort: "In your opinion, what is the most beautiful mathematical equation?" or "This space is blank. Please fill it with something that will improve the void." People who lack the patience to "improve the gap" don't qualify but those who understand the question and find it interesting are exactly the type of people Google wants to hire.

Another technique for finding people with innovative potential is the Google Code Jam, a contest where participants compete online to solve the same problems in a given time. The prize is $10,000 and a job offer from Google. At Code Jam 2006 there were job offers for the first 20 finalists, and 21,000 people from all over the world competed.[144] The winners came from Russia, Poland and China, showing that Google draws on global talent. Participants for Code Jam 2010 came from 125 countries. The top 100 went to a final test at Google headquarters where they had to show more creativity: each contestant had to try to break the software code of the other participants.

Google also has a program for young managers (Associate Product Manager), which rewards innovation, regardless of age, by placing employees in leadership positions early on. For example, Brian Rakowski, was put in charge of launching Gmail, when he was only 22 years old.[145]

At Apple they wait as long as necessary until they find the ideal candidate. According to a former Apple recruiter (Sharon Aby), "I fought with some managers who wanted to fill a role quickly to get a project moving, but if it took six months to find the best, they´d have to wait. We looked for people who were excited to create new things. Our motto was 'Surprise me'."[146] Jobs told those who wanted to work at Apple, "Our heroes are innovators. We stand for innovation. If you want to work at Apple, we expect you to be an innovator who wants to change the world."[147] One of the things Jobs did when he returned to Apple in 1997, 12 years after being fired, is the famous "Think different" advertisemnt that said,

Here´s to the crazy ones. The misfits. The rebels. The trouble makers... the ones who see things differently. They're not fond of rules. And they have no respect for the status quo... they change things. They push the human race forward.[148]

The idea of the ad was to remind all employees and customers that Apple was going to drive innovation. This ad won an Emmy Award. The whole point of the 'Think Different' campaign was that people had forgotten what Apple stood for, including employees. With the return of Jobs, Apple innovated again. Of course, these statements in favour of innovation must be supported with concrete actions. Alan G. Lafley (former CEO of P&G) said,

The P&G of five or six years ago depended on eight thousand scientists and engineers for the vast majority of innovations. The P&G we are trying to unleash today asks all hundred thousand-plus of us to be innovators.[149]

To make it a reality, he asked all areas of the company for new ideas and if these were promising, he put them into development. For example, he supported a line of hair products for women of colour because African American employees explained to him that traditional products did not work well and that they "could do better." This is how the new shampoo line, Pantene Pro-V Relax & Natural, was born. Lafley thus created an environment favourable to innovation.

At Amazon people like inventing things and, as a result, other people who like inventing are attracted there. Bezos says that if people don't like to invent, they feel uncomfortable at Amazon. It's like a virtuous circle that reinforces itself. In interviews with potential employees, Bezos asked, "Tell me about something that you've invented."[150] The invention can be something small, like a new addition to a product or a process that improves the customer experience, or a new way to load the dishwasher. But what he wants to know is whether the interviewee is capable of trying something new.[151] Bezos supported the implementation of the *Just Do It!* award, for anyone who improves or invents a process or product – without prior authorization from their boss – that improves the experience of Amazon customers. The award is presented by him in person.

Innovative companies promote a culture of innovation by giving their people time and resources to try out new things. Ronald Mitsch, a former vice president of Research and Development at 3M – the company that invented Scotch tape in 1925 and Post-it notes in 1980 – explains, that Innovation doesn't happen unless you assure your people that it is a priority and you provide them with "enough freedom" and resources to develop it.[152] In 1920, 3M instituted the practice of giving 15% of free time to its staff to develop products of interest to them and from this time Arthur Fry's Post-It Notes emerged. 3M strives to make 25% of its sales come from products that did not exist 5 years before. It also awards prizes for innovation, such as the *Golden Step Award* created in 1972. More than 6,000 employees have won "Golden Step awards as members of new product teams."[153] The team that developed Post-it won this award.

Google gives its employees 20 percent of free time to undertake projects of interest, in addition to other benefits such as hair salons, gyms, laundromats, childcare centers, car cleaning, gourmet food in different restaurants and cafes, transport to the Google campus, health insurance, retirement, etc. –all of which facilitates work and innovation. From this 20 percent of free time came some of the most successful products: Gmail, Google News, AdSense and Orkut (a popular social network in Brazil). Scientist Krishna Bharat, a Google employee frustrated by how difficult it was to find news online, created Google News in his 20 percent of his free time. The site now receives millions of visits daily.[154]

Also from these experiments emerged Google Talk (the instant messaging application), Google Sky (which allows users interested in astronomy to browse images of the universe), and Google Translate (the language translation software). Engineer Alec Proudfoot, whose 20 percent project was aimed at increasing the efficiency of hybrid cars, said in a television interview, "Just about all the good ideas here at Google have bubbled up from 20 percent time."[155]

This is not something that happens only at Google. At P&G, some employees said they were encouraged to spend 75 percent of their time working "within the system" (on delivery and executive tasks) and 25 percent working "above the system" (for example, figuring out better ways of performing some process).[156] Other companies, such as Apple and Amazon, do not give an explicit time allocation, but regularly ask employees to conduct experiments and work on innovative projects.

In conclusion, the book *The Innovator's DNA* has a confusing title because DNA refers to genes. But as we can see, the reason why these famous innovators discover good ideas is not due to their genes but to their behaviours in questioning, observing, experimenting and networking. This implies that any of us can increase our creativity if we put these behaviours into practice, like the executive who began to practice them and was soon promoted to the strategic planning unit. The researchers say the study revealed that the ability to generate ideas is not only a function of the mind but also a function of these behaviours. This is good news for everyone because it means that "if we change our behaviour, we can improve our creativity." In short, the key is in our *action* and not just in our thought.

Never give up

What is notable about these innovators is their courage and the effort they make to carry out their ventures. An example of this is Fred Smith, founder of Federal Express. In 1971 Smith founded this fabulous company that delivers mail and packages within 24-48 hours. But it was not until July 1975 that he had his first profitable month. The obstacles he had to overcome were many. By 1972 Smith had managed to raise $52 million in financing to purchase airplanes and make other investments. But his time was taken up trying to raise more funds and dealing with impatient investors who threatened to sue him and foreclose on his debt. Smith describes these difficult times,

No man on earth will ever know all I went through during that year. With the trauma of that year, the great pressure I felt on my shoulders, so many things happening at the same time, so many trips and meetings with bankers, investors (...) hundreds of different people who came to see me in Memphis –I can't remember the details of that period. At the same time I had to run a company.[157]

Smith had to negotiate with government officials to obtain more flexible regulations, manage modifications in the weight of the planes, obtain gasoline during the oil embargo of those years, as well as supervise the training of pilots, truck drivers, salespeople, managers and administrative personnel. He could not offer these people good salaries but only the hope of a better future. On top of that he had to get clients. Art Bass, former president of Federal Express, remembers that the company should have gone bankrupt 5 or 6 times in the first three or four years but Smith did not give up. He was tenacious. "With the courage of a bull, he managed to pull off a miracle. That's the only way to express what Smith did."[158]

Psychologist Angela Duckworth (University of Pennsylvania) studied young people who entered the West Point military school to undergo highly demanding training.[159] She also analysed groups of students, entrepreneurs, athletes and famous actors, etc. In each case it was *perseverance that predicted success, not talent or creativity*. The determining factor for innovation is not intelligence but what each person *does with it*. One may have a lot of creativity, but then just sit back without ever trying.

There are those with intelligence and creativity who have not achieved much because they have not worked as hard as Smith, or Jobs or others. The professors who wrote *The Innovator's DNA* asked Elon Musk, founder of Tesla, "What would you recommend to people who want to be innovators?" Elon replied: "I would ask them how hard they have tried. Creativity and innovation take time. It takes effort. A lot of people want it to happen but they're not really willing to put in the time and effort."[160]

DIEGO F. WARTJES

> Leadership is like holding a dove in your hand. If you press too hard, you may kill it, but if you hold it too gently, you may lose it.[161]
>
> Tommy Lassorda
> (Dodgers chief)

Chapter 4

What does being a "good boss" mean?

Leadership is a topic of transcendental importance today. Not only in business life but in politics –for example, for presidents, armies, in sports, religion, family, etc. In his book *Good Boss, Bad Boss*, Sutton says a great leader has two traits: *professionalism* and *humanity* (treating others well); that is, working well but also being humane. The ideal boss is one who treats employees with respect and makes them grow professionally. He does things in a way that increases, rather than destroys, the dignity and pride of their people. Studies on hunting tribes and modern groups conclude that effective leaders are 'competent and benevolent'.[162]

However, when stories about leaders appear in the press, very often there is a focus on charisma, on how dazzling or likable this or that company president is. But since studies and surveys started on employees about the type of boss they would work for again, it is not the charismatic ones but the ones who did *what had to be done under the circumstances*. That is, those who were not afraid to make difficult decisions, those who knew when to put on pressure and when to give their people more freedom, those who did not avoid "the dirty work", like summoning an employee to their office and explaining that they are harming the team's work with their attitudes.

According to Daniel Ames and Frank Flynn (Columbia University), many bosses do not know when they are pushing their people too hard or not pushing them hard enough. Bosses who put too much pressure on their employees damage work relationships. But those who do not put enough pressure do not achieve much. Finding the right balance is therefore vital to being a good boss. With this in mind, they hypothesized that the best bosses would be valued by their staff as *decisive, fair and responsible* people, that is, bosses who face problems and try to solve them with courage and determination. Well then, when 213 business school students were asked to rate their most recent bosses, the highest rated were those bosses described as determined and responsible. The students also said they would be happy to work for them again.[163]

Now, in the world of innovation, the fundamental trait of leadership is to give the team freedom to act on their own, without the need for prior permissions. Clarifying this is important because there are many executives who think that the more pressure they apply, the better it is, but for innovation —says Sutton— this attitude is negative. There are several studies that show that in the most innovative teams, bosses lead people with less supervision, allowing them to act without permission. For instance, Anne Cummings and Greg Oldham studied 171 workers at an industrial plant, comparing those with highly controlling bosses to those with low-controlling bosses. Workers with less-than-controlling bosses made the most novel suggestions.[164] Researchers at Cornell University studied 320 small businesses, half of which gave their workers *autonomy*, while the other half were under their bosses' *strict control*. Business in companies that gave their employees autonomy grew four times more than in those that exercised strict control.[165]

Michael Kirton carried out a series of studies comparing the style of people he calls *adaptive* (who adapt and make small improvements but always within structured frameworks) with the style of *innovative* people, those who *totally ignore structures* and re-frame problems, looking at them from original points of view. He used a 32-question survey and discovered that people who completely ignore structures and act without asking permission from bosses have more novel ideas than those with an adaptive style.[166]

In the business world there are several cases of bosses and managers who applied this attitude of little supervision and managed to boost innovation in their teams. Will Coyne headed 3M's research and development division. For more than a decade, he did his work guided by this wise quote, "After you plant a seed in the ground, you don't dig it up every week to see how it's doing."[167] Part of his job was to keep intruders away from his team so they could work in peace. Part of this creative freedom policy is the *15% rule* or "Friday afternoon experiments," which allows 3M employees to work on their own experiments.

A 3M director saw a scientist asleep under his bench and threatened to fire him. But Coyne took this director to the "Patent Wall of Inventions" and showed him that the scientist had developed some of the company's most profitable products and then advised him, "Next time you see him asleep, give him a pillow."[168] Another example dates back to 1925 when then-CEO William McKnight ordered an employee, Richard Drew, to stop working on a project he considered "silly" and return to his quality control job. Drew ignored him and continued developing *Scotch Tape*, one of 3M's most successful products. Despite this negative order of McKnight's, it is fair to remember that it was he who instituted the 15% rule that led to the creation of several innovative 3M products.

David Packard, co-founder of Hewlett & Packard (HP), comments in his biography that a few years before, at the HP laboratory in Colorado Springs dedicated to oscilloscope technology, one of the engineers, Chuck House, was ordered to abandon a display monitor he was developing. But House ignored the order and went off on a vacation to California, stopping along the way to show potential customers a prototype of his monitor. He wanted to know what they thought, what they wanted the product to do, and what its limitations were. The positive reactions prompted him to continue with the project, although upon his return, he discovered that Packard had suspended the project. House persuaded his boss to speed up production of the monitor, and as a result, HP sold more than 17,000 display monitors, generating $35 million in revenue for the company.

A few years later, at an HP meeting, Packard presented Chuck with a medal for "his extraordinary contempt and defiance above and beyond the normal call of engineering duty."[169] In short, according to studies and these examples, the rule –for innovative work– is *not to control too much*, but to create an area of freedom and independence. In other words, not to do "micro-management" but to give general guidelines and supervise *from a distance*. A leader's job should be to ensure that his team can work on his behalf. As we can see, the most advisable management style is "laissez-faire management", a work environment with much more freedom than under traditional management.

Psychological safety

Another more current example of this management style is Brad Bird. Pixar's first three films were *Toy Story 1, Toy Story 2* and *A Bug's Life*, all of which were highly successful. Having achieved these successes, Pixar's directors (Steve Jobs, John Lasseter and Ed Catmull) were worried they might relax and slip into mediocrity. They feared complacency, the feeling that they had already made it to the top. So they set out to find the most difficult and most talented person they knew and that was Brad Bird. They said, "Go ahead, mess with our heads, shake it up."[170] Bird is not difficult as a boss but as an employee. He had been fired from Disney and *The Simpsons* show for questioning his bosses and complaining about the mediocrity to which, in his view, these companies' products had fallen.

However, as a boss he knew how to create an environment where workers felt safe to speak their minds at all times. Bird says that before coming to Pixar, he was at Warners Bros remaking a film, *Iron Giant*, which subsequently received good reviews but did not do so well commercially. When he arrived at the first meeting at Warner, the workers looked like a group of "abused" children, afraid to give their opinion. So Bird gave a motivational speech: "I'm going to take a shot at what I think will improve a scene, but if you see something different, go ahead and disagree. I don't´t know all the answers."[171]

However, everyone remained silent for a couple of months until one day he drew something on the board. "I think the elbow needs to come up higher here so that we feel the thrust of this action. Does anybody disagree? Come on, speak up." One of the guys sighed and Bird shouted, "What was that?" And this guy said, "Nothing man, it's OK." And Bird said, "No, you *sighed*. Clearly, you disagree with something I did there. Show me what you're thinking. I might not have it right."

This guy came up, erased what Bird did and did something different. Bird then said, "That's better than what I did. Great." Everybody saw that he didn't get his head chopped off. And in this way, the team's work began to improve. This action by Bird is called creating "psychological safety," a *work environment characterized by interpersonal trust and mutual respect* where people feel comfortable being themselves, a climate where they can speak out "without fear of being ridiculed or punished."[172]

Harvard Professor Amy Edmondson did a study on 26 nurses in 9 hospitals and discovered that the best nurse teams are those where managers encourage them to give their opinions freely. Those teams detected and reported ten times more errors than teams with fear-inspiring bosses who treated nurses like "two-year-olds."[173]

In the Xerox Parc research and development laboratory (where the first mouse and the graphics user interface were invented) there was this environment of *psychological safety*. One of the bosses, Bob Taylor, had an attitude that made everyone feel safe and able to put aside their fears and egos to focus on solving problems.[174] He promoted the free discussion of ideas and open criticism, but not with the aim of giving his workers a hard time but rather to motivate and inspire them to have better ideas.

This environment placed innovation at the center of the laboratory, leaving politics and hierarchies aside. John Mauchly, who together with John Prespert Eckert Jr. invented the first computer in history, the Eniac (which we said weighed 30 tons), also created an environment of psychological safety at the University of Pennsylvania —where this computer was invented— and also in his company, the Eckert-Mauchly Computer Corporation. Grace Hopper, one of the Eniac programmers, pointed out that Mauchly "let people try things out. He encouraged innovation." [175]

In *Innovation and the Innovative Entrepreneur* (1987), Peter Drucker, the "father of management," gives his advice: "To allow it to innovate, a business has to be able to *free* its best performers for the challenges of innovation."[176] In his vision, the boss should organise informal meetings with employees and start them with these words,

> I'm not here to make a speech or to tell you anything. I'm here to listen. I want to hear from you what your aspirations are, but above all, where you see opportunities for this company and where you see threats. And what are your ideas for us to try to do new things.[177]

> This kind of meetings must be organized regularly because they are an excellent vehicle for upward communication, the best means to enable juniors, and especially professionals, to look up from their narrow specialities and see the whole enterprise. They enable juniors to understand what top management is concerned with, and why. In turn, they give the senior badly needed insight into the values, vision and concerns of their younger colleagues.[178]

Psychological safety in Google teams

Google researchers did a research called *Project Aristotle* where they discovered that psychological safety is the most important ingredient of the best work teams.[179] To find out why some groups of people stand out and others do not, they reviewed half a century of academic studies and analysed how teams worked. Based on those studies, they asked, How often do Google team members socialise outside the office? Do they have the same hobbies? Are their educational backgrounds similar? Is it better for members to be outgoing or shy? Are the best teams made up of people with similar interests? Or does it matter more if everyone is motivated by the same type of rewards?

However, no matter how they organized the data, it was nearly impossible to find patterns or any evidence that a team's composition made a difference. "We analyzed 180 work teams. We had a lot of data, but there was nothing to show that a combination of personality types or specific skills or backgrounds made any difference," says Abeer Dubey, manager of Google's People's Analytics division. The "who" part of the team didn't seem to matter. Some of Google's most efficient teams were made up of friends who socialized outside of work while others were made up of people who did not hang out after work. Some teams were looking for strong managers while others preferred open and flexible bosses. "At Google, we are good at finding patterns," Dubey notes, yet "there were no clear patterns here."

In 2008 a group of psychologists from Carnegie Mellon, M.I.T. and Union College began to research the formula or the secrets of the best work teams.[180] These psychologists wanted to know if there was a *collective intelligence* different from the intelligence of each team member. To do this, they recruited 699 people, divided them into small groups and assigned them a series of tasks that required collaboration. One of the tasks, for example, consisted in participants brainstorming possible uses for a brick. Another was to coordinate a shopping trip where each member was responsible for a different grocery list. The researchers concluded that what distinguishes "good" teams is *how members treat each other*. They noticed two behaviors that best teams share.

Firstly, all members *spoke for approximately the same amount of time,* a phenomenon that researchers call "equality in the distribution of conversational turns." In some teams, everyone talked during each task; in others, leadership changed depending on the given task. But at the end of the day, everyone had talked for about the same length of time. "As long as everyone had a chance to weigh in, the team did well," notes Anita Woolley, lead author of the Carnegie Melon study. "But if only one person or a small group spoke all the time, collective intelligence decreased." Secondly, the best teams had high "average social sensitivity"—that is, their members were skilled at sensing how others were feeling *based on their tone of voice, gestures, and other nonverbal cues.*

One of the easiest ways to measure *social sensitivity* is to show someone photos of other people's eyes and ask them to describe what they are thinking or feeling, a test known as *Reading the Mind in the Eyes*. The best teams in Woolley's experiment scored above average on this test. They seemed to know when a classmate was feeling upset or left out by looking at their face and expressions. This is decisive for people understanding each other given that up to 98% of communication is non-verbal. You can say "Thank you very much" with a smile or with a sarcastic expression, which completely changes the meaning of the words. The least effective teams, in contrast, scored below average; they seemed to have less sensitivity toward their colleagues. In psychology, researchers refer to "conversational turns" and "average social sensitivity" as aspects of *psychological safety*.

The conclusion of *Project Aristotle* is that who is on a team matters less than *how they interact*, the way they structure their work, and recognise each other's contributions. This project also discovered that, in addition to psychological safety, there are other behaviours important to team effectiveness such as *reliability*, which was analyzed based on the question, "Can we count on each other to do quality work on time?" The *structure* and *clarity* of the objectives was analyzed based on the question, "Does our team have clear objectives, roles and execution plans?" The *meaning of work*: "Are we working on something that is personally important to each of us?" and *the impact of the task*: "Do we believe that the work we are doing will have an impact on other people?"

Psychological safety was analyzed based on the question, "Can we take risks in this team without fear of being humiliated or disqualified?" If a team answers "yes" to these questions, it is probably performing well, and if not, these questions can guide us to reflect on how to do better. This study also found that those on psychologically safe teams are *less* likely to quit Google, are more likely to leverage their colleagues' ideas, and generate more revenue.[181] To foster psychological safety, researchers created a tool called *gTeams* that consists of three steps: i) a 10-minute assessment of team behaviours, ii) a report summarising how the team is performing, and iii) a conversation to discuss results and help teams improve. More than 3,000 Googlers across 300 teams have used this tool, and teams that took action improved 6% in psychological safety scores and 10% in structure and goal clarity scores. The *Aristotle Project* has fostered conversations and discussions about how teams work and how people feel that would not otherwise come to light. Matt Sakaguchi, Google manager comments,

> By putting things like *empathy* and *sensitivity* into charts and data reports, it makes them easier to talk about. 'It's easier to talk about our feelings when we can point to a number.[182]

Power distance and individualism

Two other concepts closely related to psychological safety are what sociologists and psychologists call *power distance and individualism*. Power distance is the relationship with authority, that is, the way those who *have power in a society treat others*, while individualism is the relationship of the individual with society, in other words, *the degree of autonomy or freedom that each society grants to the individual* (*individualism* is measured in opposition to *collectivism*, when the degree of autonomy is low).

According to studies by Dutch anthropologist, psychologist and engineer Geer Hofstede, in organisations and societies with *long* power distance, employees are more afraid of expressing disagreements with their bosses than in those with *short* power distance.[183] In those with *long* power distance, command is usually hierarchical and vertical; there is a reverential fear of authority, be it of one's boss, one's father's or of the State.

Power is based on connections, strength or wealth: the assumption is that those who have power must have privileges. Therefore, an individual with an innovative idea may feel inhibited from proposing it to his boss. These organizations and societies also have a low degree of individualism or, conversely, a high degree of *collectivism*: the *opinion of the majority* is valued above that of the individual. For example, if within a work group an individual has an interesting proposal but their group mostly holds with the opposite, the group's opinion is more likely to prevail. A majority criterion is therefore applied, instead of analysing whether the proposal itself is good or bad.

On the other hand, in *short* power distance organizations and societies, communication between employees and bosses is more direct, which facilitates the circulation of ideas. Employees easily approach their bosses and contradict them. Command is usually more open and flexible, consultative in style. The common belief is that everyone should have the same rights regardless of the position they hold. Power is based on *merit* and *skill*. Therefore, if an individual has an innovative proposal they may feel quite at ease discussing it with their boss.

They also have a greater degree of *individualism*, that is, respect for the individual as long as it does not affect the rights of third parties. For instance, if an individual has an innovative proposal, they are more likely to be listened to and have their idea analysed to verify whether it is good or not in itself, as opposed to automatically applying what the majority thinks. Individualism is also synonymous with *individual freedom*. And according to the studies of anthropologist Homer G.

Barnett, there is a "positive correlation between individualism and innovative potential." The greater the freedom of individuals to explore their world of experiences and to organise the elements according to their personal interpretation, "the greater the likelihood that new ideas will arise." [184] What are the *short* and *long* distance power societies?

Those with *short* power distance —with open and consultative command— are, for example, the United States, the United Kingdom, Canada, Germany, Holland, Switzerland, Sweden, Denmark, Finland and Israel, countries that have a high level of innovation if we take into account typical indicators such as the number of invention patents and innovative companies (all countries measured are listed below). Likewise, there are several studies that show that a *short* power distance and a greater degree of individualism *correlate with a greater number of invention patents*.[185] On the other hand, societies with *long* distance to power —with hierarchical and vertical command— are the Latin American, African and Arab, all in process of development and with lower levels of innovation.

Now then, innovators stand out for behaving and thinking differently from the majority; they often have a rebellious personality. Steve Jobs' motto as we have seen was, "Here´s to the crazy ones. The misfits. The rebels. The trouble makers.." When Bill Gates' mother —a strong-willed woman— would call Bill for dinner, he was in the basement where he had his bedroom and would not answer. "What are you doing?" his mother once asked him. "I'm thinking," Bill shouted in response. "You are thinking?" said the mother. "Yes, mom, I'm thinking. Have you ever tried doing it?" His mother took him to see a psychologist who, after a year of therapy, said to her, "You have everything to lose... it's not worth trying to change him." A professor of Larry Page and Sergey Brin (founders of Google), remembers that "They had no respect for authority. They spent their time challenging me. They had no qualms about saying to me, 'You're just talking nonsense!'"[186]

This sort of individuals do not usually follow tradition or customs. On the contrary, they deviate from them to do something new. The problem is that to diverge they need freedom of action. In which countries are they most likely to find this freedom? Evidently in those with *short power distance* –with open, flexible command rather than hierarchical– and with a *high degree of individualism*. In short, where their creativity and rebellion are not hindered or bogged down by an autocratic boss or by the pressure of the majority.

Below are the country scores on the Hofstede scales, with high values where power distance is *long* and lower when it is shorter. Brazil and Argentina, for example, appear with a score of 69 and 49 respectively, which reveals a longer power distance than in the United States and the Netherlands, with 40 and 38 respectively. If we go by these scores, in Brazilian and Argentine societies there would be a greater fear of expressing disagreement with bosses or proposing something innovative than in American and Dutch societies.[187] Note also the scores for India and China since many engineers working in Silicon Valley come from these countries (we mentioned at the beginning that a great part of the technological talent in S. Valley comes from India and China).

Country scores on power distance

COUNTRY	POWER DISTANCE
Malaysia	104
Slovakia	104
Guatemala	95
Panama	95
Philippines	94
Russia	93
Romania	90
Serbia	86
Surinam	85
Mexico	81
Venezuela	81
Arab countries (e.g. Egypt and Saudi Arabia)	80
Bangladesh	80
China	**80**
Ecuador	78
Indonesia	78
India	**77**
West African countries (e.g. Nigeria and Ghana)	77
Singapore	74
Croatia	73
Slovenia	71
Bulgaria	70
Morocco	70
French speaking Switzerland	70
Vietnam	70
Brazil	**69**
France	68
Hong Kong	68
Poland	68

COUNTRY	POWER DISTANCE
French speaking Belgium	67
Colombia	67
El Salvador	66
Türkiye	66
East African countries (e.g. Tanzania and Ethiopia)	64
Peru	64
Thailand	64
Chili	63
Portugal	63
Dutch speaking Belgium	61
Uruguay	61
Greece	61
South Korea	60
Iran	58
Taiwan	58
Czech Republic	57
Spain	57
Malt	56
Pakistan	55
Canada	54
Japan	54
Italy	50
Argentina	**49**
S. Africa	49
Trinity	47
Hungary	46
Jamaica	45
Latvia	44
Lithuania	42
Estonia	40
Luxembourg	40
USA	**40**
Canada	39

COUNTRY	POWER DISTANCE
Netherlands	**38**
Australia	36
Costa Rica	35
Germany	35
United Kingdom	35
Finland	33
Norway	31
Sweden	31
Ireland	28
German speaking Switzerland	26
New Zealand	22
Denmark	18
Israel	13
Austria	11

Next, the Hofstede *individualism* scale, with higher scores where there is more individualism (or less collectivism). The United States and Netherlands appear with scores of 91 and 80, which shows much more individualism than in Brazil and Argentina, with 38 and 46 respectively. If we go by these scores, in Brazilian and Argentine societies adopting the group's decision is more common than adopting the individual's even when the individual has a more innovative proposal or a better idea than the group's, compared to American and Dutch societies.[188] Note also the scores for India and China.

Individualism scores

COUNTRY	INDIVIDUALISM
USA	91
Australia	90
United Kingdom	89
Canada	80
Hungary	80

COUNTRY	INDIVIDUALISM
Netherlands	**80**
New Zealand	79
Dutch speaking Belgium	78
Italy	76
Denmark	74
Canada Quebec	73
French speaking Belgium	72
France	71
Sweden	71
Ireland	70
Latvia	70
Norway	69
German speaking Switzerland	69
Germany	67
South Africa	65
French speaking Switzerland	64
Finland	63
Estonia	60
Lithuania	60
Luxembourg	60
Poland	60
Malt	59
Czech Republic	58
Austria	55
Israel	54
Slovakia	52
Spain	51
India	**48**
Surinam	47

COUNTRY	INDIVIDUALISM
Argentina	**46**
Japan	46
Morocco	46
Iran	41
Jamaica	39
Russia	39
Arabian countries	38
Brazil	**38**
Türkiye	37
Uruguay	36
Greece	35
Croatia	33
Philippines	32
Bulgaria	30
Mexico	30
Romania	30
East African countries	27
Portugal	27
Slovenia	27
Malaysia	26
Hong Kong	25
Serbia	25
Chili	23
Bangladesh	20
China	**20**
Singapore	20
Thailand	20
Vietnam	20
West African countries	20

COUNTRY	INDIVIDUALISM
El Salvador	19
South Korea	18
Taiwan	17
Peru	16
Trinity	16
Costa Rica	15
Indonesia	14
Pakistan	14
Colombia	13
Venezuela	12
Panama	11
Ecuador	8
Guatemala	6

Being in tune with the people you lead

According to psychological studies, we humans have a natural tendency to believe that we are better than we really are. This can be seen in everyday things like believing we drive better than we do. In a US study of car drivers, 90% of respondents claimed they had "above average" driving skills. This also happens with leadership. In a survey of nearly a million high school students, 70% reported having "above average" leadership skills and only 2% believed they were "below average." What's more, research shows that the most incompetent people rate themselves the highest. This tendency is called "self enhancement bias" –something like "self-aggrandizement bias."[189]

However, it is colleagues, superiors and clients who can offer a better assessment of our strengths and weaknesses. A study of naval officers found that peer ratings were the best predictors of who would be promoted, not the self-evaluations. This bias is therefore an obstacle to improvement and applies to all areas of life: business, politics, sports, music, hobbies, and so on. If Federer, Djokovic or Nadal were guided by this bias, they would not continue to win such a number of tennis tournaments. They are obsessed with improving. Well, good bosses also have this obsession. They are constantly concerned about perfecting their leadership skills and to do so they seek to be *in tune with their team*: they want to know the effect their words have on others and understand the strengths and weaknesses of the people they work with to get the best out of them.

Many say that Steve Jobs had a difficult personality but, according to people who worked with him, he had the ability to understand what people's strengths and weaknesses were and how to lead them to get the best out of them. This type of leadership only occurs when bosses are in tune with the people they lead, when they know how to motivate each worker according to their personality, since not everyone reacts in the same way to a given kind of motivation. There are those who work very well under pressure while others need praise or constant support from their boss. To be a good leader one needs to be a good "psychologist" in the sense of understanding the personality of each member of a team, knowing how to interpret their gestures, tones of voice and situations.

Former General Electric CEO Jack Welch says that being a boss "It's not about you", "When you were made a leader, you are not given a crown; you were given the responsibility to bring out the best in others."[190] However, there are two exceptions —says Sutton— where it is exclusively about the boss. The first is that bosses are automatically assigned more than 50% of the responsibility for the teams' success or failure, whether fair or unfair.[191] Therefore, part of a boss's job is to deal with this exclusive attribution of responsibility. The second is that the people on a team observe their boss much more than the boss observes them, which is natural since the boss has control of their lives and careers.

Anthropologists and ethologists say that the average member of a troop of gorillas or baboon monkeys looks at the alpha male —the boss— every twenty or thirty seconds but the other way round does not occur as regularly.¹⁹² This is what happens to those in a position of authority or leadership: their people are constantly paying attention to them. The problem is that there is a tendency for bosses not to pay enough attention to their team. Therefore, they can easily fall out of tune, not knowing what is happening with their people.

Sutton tells of a boss who was completely surprised when a secretary discovered a well-kept secret: that there would be layoffs. The secretary approached him one day and asked, "There are going to be layoffs, right?" and the boss replied, "Yes, ther will be layoffs, but how do you know since no one in the company knows, except for some managers and shareholders?" She explained that when there were problems, he didn't look people in the eye but down at his feet. This situation shows that employees and secretaries usually know much more about their bosses' behaviour than they know about themselves or their teams. People watch everything bosses do and learn to read their gestures, the tapping of fingers when they are impatient or the raising of eyebrows before interrupting someone else's explanation. They talk about their behaviours when they are not there and assign meaning to everything they do.¹⁹³

A final example is Linda Hudson, CEO of BAE Systems. After getting a big promotion, she realised that people were watching every little thing she did. A week before said promotion, she bought a scarf and the saleswoman showed her how to tie it in a different way than the usual. At the end of her first week on the job, she looked around and there were many women in her office with scarfs tied just like hers.¹⁹⁴ In short, when one is in a leadership position, the focus of attention is on the leader, noticing everything they do, say or fail to do. But since this attention is not reciprocal, one of the main challenges of a good boss is not to fall out of *tune with their team*.

The cookie experiment

The tendency of many bosses to not pay attention to those in their charge is made worse by the effect that arises when someone is given power. Almost everyone knows the saying, "If you want to test a man's character, give him power." A large body of research —says Sutton— shows that when people are put in positions of power, they tend to focus more on their own needs, to care less about the needs of others and to act as if the rules did not apply to them. To demonstrate this, research was done at the University of California, Berkeley. Three students were placed in a room. Two of them were given the job of writing an essay proposing public measures, that is, small things like what we could do to dispose of garbage faster, what to do to make the university campus have more green spaces, etc. The third was appointed "boss" and assigned the task of evaluating the ideas of the other two and also paying them.

After 30 minutes, the experimenter entered the room and placed a plate with five cookies on the table where these three students were. Anyone familiar with psychological experiments knows that psychologists use different methods to manipulate people in their studies. The plan was to see who would take the last cookie —as we all know, it is not good manners to take the last one for oneself. It turns out that the student who had been named "boss" not only took the last cookie but also chewed with his mouth open and left more crumbs than the others.[195]

In short, when people are in positions of power, i) they focus more on their concerns and desires, ii) they care less about the problems of others, and iii) they act as if the rules did not apply to them. Therefore, to be a good boss, you have to be in tune with the people you lead because it has been proven that a position of power leads people to be more careless and abusive in their relationships with others. Good leaders fight against these tendencies and this is vital to becoming an effective head of innovation. In 1958, David Packard advised his managers,

> Take care with the little details. Watch your smile, your tone of voice, how you use your eyes, the way you greet people, the use of nicknames and remembering faces, names and dates. Little things add polish to your skill in dealing with people.

Constantly, deliberately think of them until they become a natural part of your personality.[196]

The small steps strategy

Another important aspect for leadership is to adopt a small steps strategy. According to Jim Collins' studies, good leaders often have big goals or big ideas about how to build innovative products. Thinking big motivates people (Collins is the author of *From Good to Great*). But there are also studies that say that if a team is presented with big goals but are not shown the *small steps* to achieve them, they may lose focus, become demotivated, or not know how to move forward. Teresa Amabile and Steve Kramer studied several teams for years and discovered that the key to their success was that their leaders organised their work in small steps or, as they call it, "small wins."[197]

Small steps are useful because people want to feel, *on a daily basis*, that they are doing something important or useful. For them to commit to the task, they must be able to feel they are making steady progress and not just hope to achieve a big long-term goal. It is essential for the leader to point out at the end of the year the progress made by the team as well as those who have contributed to make it happen. This encourages people psychologically and motivates them to achieve more things the following year. They also advise to plan goals for the next year and explain why that progress is important, making sure to include great, ambitious goals but also *intermediate* and *small* ones.

Alcoholics Anonymous associations have been successful in helping alcoholics because instead of insisting that they become completely abstemious for the rest of their lives, they encourage them to remain sober *one day at a time*, or one hour at a time. The impossibility of lifelong abstinence is therefore reduced to the most feasible goal: not drinking for 24 hours, or a week. Several studies on micro-innovation demonstrate the effectiveness of taking small steps. For instance, a study of reductions in production costs at five DuPont plants between 1929 and 1960 shows that small technical changes, rather than major changes, accounted for more than two-thirds of the cost reduction.[198] This reduction was the product of small inventions made by workers familiar with the daily operations.

It is natural to applaud the great invention while overlooking the small steps. However, it is by no means true that the increase in productivity is mainly due to great inventions. It may well be that the sum total of "small improvements, each too small to be called an invention, has contributed to the increase in productivity more than the great inventions have."[199] Small steps are also easier to take and more stable. This characteristic is illustrated by counting 1,000 sheets of paper. When someone interrupts a count of 1,000 sheets, they are forced to start over if they did not retain the last number. On the other hand, if the sheets are counted and placed in piles of 100, not only is much less counting time wasted but, in the event of interruptions, the chances of easily resuming the count are much higher. The short stacks of leaves are then like the small victories or steps, on the way to the big goal.

In short, when leading a team it is advisable to divide the big objective into small steps and create the conditions so that the team can make it on their own. The *Tao Te Ching* quote, "A journey of a thousand miles begins with a single step," is something we apply in our daily lives as we accomplish our big goals in steps, be it a long-term career, a promotion, a college degree, a positive relationship with our partner, etc. The path to final success is taken day by day. And if you think in terms of how much time should be spent thinking about the big goals versus the small steps, the formula would be 1% of the time thinking about the great goals, yet 99% of the time thinking about the small steps that will make it possible.

Sutton recalled that at the end of 2008 the CEO of a software company in America was told that if she did not achieve a sales increase of at least 35% more than the previous year, there would be many layoffs in her division. She approached her team and gave them this bad news. As expected, everyone became quite nervous and started complaining, worried about how they were going to achieve this goal in a recessionary economy. However, she said, "Wait, don't be scared! Let's break this down into small steps." So she took a lot of Post-its and handed them out to her team and said, "Start writing down all the little steps we need to take to achieve the goal of increasing sales by 35%." Soon she collected about 100 Post-its with small goals, drew a line down a whiteboard and placed 60 of them on the easy side and 40 on the hard-to-achieve part. She then said, "Let's think about what we can do to achieve the easiest ones as quickly as possible."[200]

Within two weeks it turned out that the team had achieved all the easy ones and that gave them the energy and optimism to face the more difficult ones. By dividing the large goal into small steps, the CEO and her team avoided a large number of layoffs. The point is that when she told them about the large goal, the employees were scared. But when she broke it down into manageable chunks, two good things happened: their anxiety decreased, and they realised that reaching their goal only took small steps.

Protect their backs

This last principle of good leadership is especially important, another of the hallmarks of a great leader. In different surveys people were asked what an effective boss was, who they would like to work for, etc. What people answered was that they wanted "a boss who watches my back." This means bosses who protect their team from all kinds of things, from meaningless interruptions and annoying bureaucratic requests, to abuses of power and disrespect that make life more difficult. The best bosses let their people do their jobs. They protect their teams from annoying visitors, unnecessary meetings and other time wasters. Sutton points out that,

> A good boss takes pride in serving as a human shield, absorbing and deflecting heat from superiors and customers, doing all manner of boring and silly tasks, and battling back

against every idiot and slight that makes life unfair or harder than necessary on his or her changes.[201]

According to Henry Mintzberg —one of the best management theorists of our time— the "perfect manager" is the one who serves or stops visitors "so that everyone else can do their job."[202] Jobs said something similar about his work at Apple, "The people who are doing the work are the moving force behind the Macintosh. My job is to create a space for them, to clear out the rest of the organization and *keep it at bay*."[203] This protective attitude is especially important for teams that innovate, so that they are not interrupted by executives from other areas asking them to do things that are not their job or executives who bother them out of envy or jealousy, who cannot resist having employees who were once "theirs" doing innovation for another boss.

An interesting anecdote took place in the computer division of Lucasfilm, the company of George Lucas (creator of *Star Wars* movies). In 1985, Lucas hired an executive named Doug Norby as president of the division to implement some financial discipline. Norby put pressure on bosses to put together a list of workers to lay off. The bosses were Ed Catmull (the dreamer who envisioned Pixar long before it produced hit films like *Toy Story* and so many others) and Alvy Ray Smith (the inventor of the technology that made computer-animated films possible). But neither Catmull nor Smith dared to make the list of potential layoffs. They were determined to protect their team. Instead, they made a financial argument for keeping their team intact, saying that layoffs would only reduce Lucasfilm's value.

But Norby, as president, was unmoved and continued to press for a list of employees to fire. As Catmull and Smith continued to avoid him, one day Norby ordered them both to go to his office with the list of dismissals. What did these two bosses do? They showed up at his office at 9:00 and presented the list with only two names on it: Catmull and Smith. "We all kept our jobs," employee Craig Good recalls. "When word got out, we employees pooled our money to send Ed, Alvy and their wives on a thank-you night on the town."[204] This extreme protection of staff is rare, says Sutton, and sometimes it may not even be wise to attempt it. One cannot argue that every dismissal is unfair or unnecessary. But fortunately for those employees on the tightrope, a few months after this incident (1986), Steve Jobs bought Lucasfilm's computer division for 5 million dollars (and invested another 5) and renamed it Pixar. And, as the saying goes, "the rest is history." Some 30 years later, this brave gesture of protection still inspires Pixar employees.

The use of time in meetings

Finally, it is worth mentioning that work teams usually have many meetings. Unfortunately, there are bosses who use meetings to show that they are more important than the rest. Sometimes they are a little late –says Sutton– to send out the message that "the meeting can't start without me" or they keep people longer than necessary to make it clear that "I am more important than anything in your life, be it your job, your family, lunch, rest, and so on." This is usually done by bosses who are power-hungry or have big egos.

Instead, good leaders are considerate of their people and try to keep meetings as short as possible. Studies have proven that it takes people an average of 25 minutes to recover from an interruption and refocus on the task they were doing.[205] According to these studies, interruptions cut or slow down the flow of thought and divert attention to other tasks. Sometimes the most powerful businessmen are those who care the most about holding meetings on time. Andreessen-Horowitz, for example, is a successful Silicon Valley venture capital firm that invests money in start-ups and entrepreneurs. It has made billions of dollars investing in companies like Twitter and Skype. One of its partners, Ben Horowitz, says he doesn't want to be like other companies in his industry where owners "show up to meetings late then spend the entire meeting on their phones and computers." To discourage this inconsiderate behavior, Horowitz charges his partners a fine of $10 per minute when they are late for a meeting.[206] There is then a penalty for holding back young entrepreneurs who seek financing.

Another measure for effective meetings is to hold them standing up. According to studies of groups of 56 standing and 55 sitting, the groups that held meetings standing up took 34 percent less time to reach a decision.[207] There is a long history of executives having stand-up meetings, and one of the books that mentions them is *Up the Organization* by Robert Townsend, a former director of the car rental company *Avis*. According to Townsend, some meetings should be short. A good way to achieve this is to have a stand-up meeting. After a while "they get uncomfortable and can hardly wait to get the meeting over with."[208]

David Darragh, CEO of Reily (New Orleans), holds four 15-minute meetings a week. As with other activities, repetition improves results and the same applies to meetings. The role of stand-up meetings is not to talk about long-term strategic issues but to discuss issues of the day and agree who will be responsible.[209] Finally, there is research that shows that it is better for the cardiovascular system to stand (twenty or thirty minutes) than to sit, so there is also a small health benefit in this kind of meetings[210].

DIEGO F. WARTJES

> Managers who fail to share ideas
> simply do not get promoted.[211]
>
> A.G. Lafley
> (Procter & Gamble)

Chapter 5

Collaboration within the team

One of the most common misconceptions promoted by the media is that when there is great innovation, it is due to some *lone genius*, such as Thomas Edison or Steve Jobs. They are generally believed to have done everything by themselves. However, this is a myth. When we look into how innovation takes place, we almost always find that these innovators were part of teams that included very talented people. It is important then to perceive innovation as a *team effort*. In a joint interview with Steve Jobs and Bill Gates in 2007, Jobs noted,

> We were both incredibly fortunate to have good partners with whom we started companies and to have attracted wonderful people. Everything that was done at Apple and Microsoft was done by notable people.[212]

Power Point, for example, was invented by Robert Gaskins with the collaboration of Dennis Austin and Thomas Rudkin who worked for a small company –Forethought– acquired by Microsoft. After the acquisition by Microsoft, it took 3 years for PowerPoint to be ready. On Gaskins' personal blog, you can see a photo of him with his Microsoft team of some 40 people.[213] Excel was created by a team led by engineer Douglas Klunder, a Microsoft employee. "Excel was my baby," said Klunder in an interview in 2015.[214] Apple's iPod, the most successful MP3 player in history, was invented by Tony Fadell, who is considered today the inventor or "father of the iPod." Fadell was a talented engineer who had worked for Philips Electronics, where his original idea did not find any positive response from management. However, in Silicon Valley his capability came to light. Then Jon Rubinstein (Apple's hardware vice president) called him for an interview and ended up offering him a six-week contract to develop a prototype for Apple.

At Apple they thought they could make a better MP3 and asked Fadell to make some designs, describing how it could be built, what kind of components it would have, how much it would cost and all the basic research on what the *iPod* could become.[215] He designed three prototypes which he presented to Jobs and his board of executives for them to decide which of the three they would build. It was partly thanks to Fadell that Apple was able to develop the iPod in record time, just 9 months: from February to October 2001. Thomas Edison did not do things alone either: he had a famous laboratory in Menlo Park (New Jersey) with many talented people working for him. There was an intimate collaboration between Edison and his colleagues.

The Menlo Park team was composed of 14 people including Edison. Of these, 5 had a prominent role: Charles Batchelor, John Adams, John Kruesi, John Ott and Charles Wurth. Edison worked more closely with Batchelor, an Englishman whose training in mechanics and drawing complemented (and brought down to earth) Edison's crazy ideas. The relationship between Edison and Batchelor is evident in their agreement to split the profits from their inventions 50-50 and to receive shares in the companies they created. Many of the great discoveries in electricity, the telegraph or the phonograph are attributed to the ideas of Batchelor, Adams, or some of those who worked on these projects while Edison was busy making agreements with clients or looking for investors. When an experiment looked promising, Edison would not hesitate to open a new company and put together a team to carry it out.[216] Such is the case of the *Edison General*

Electric Company, known today simply as *General Electric*, where Batchelor was treasurer and general manager.

Henry Ford's is another case. What would he have been able to do without William Klann and Max Wollering? Let us remember Klan's words, "If they can kill pigs and cows that way, we can build cars that way," from which the idea of *the assembly line* arose, while Max Wollering was the inventor of the drilling, cutting and grinding tools that made it possible for the Ford Motor to produce interchangeable parts. His case also demystifies the myth of the solitary genius or superman.

In science, great ideas have also arisen from contributions of many who preceded the "lone" genius. This is true in the cases of Newton and Darwin. When Isaac Newton was asked how he came to discover the *theory of gravity*, he replied that the difficult work had been done by the Greek philosophers. Aristarchus of Samos had believed that the Earth revolved around the Sun and not the other way around; Nicholas Copernicus rediscovered the idea which had remained buried for centuries; Johannes Kepler discovered that the planets moved in elliptical –rather than circular– orbits around the Sun and Galileo perfected a telescope that allowed him to see that the orbits were indeed elliptical.

Thus, once he knew that the planets did not have a circular path but rather an elliptical one, it became evident that what moved them was the force of gravity. Newton summed it up famously, Newton summed it up famously, "I If have seen further than others, it it by standing upon the shoulders of giants."[217] Charles Darwin, author of *The Origin of Species* (1859), from which his theory of evolution emerged, also needed other people's knowledge. Darwin was a prolific letter-writer and corresponded with almost 2,000 people during his lifetime (1809-1882) to learn and gain knowledge from. There are 14,500 letters known to exist, a collection held at the University of Cambridge. These letters were "absolutely essential" to what Darwin achieved. That was how he gathered and discussed data and ideas.[218]

When large companies come up with some popular innovation, again, it is not thanks to a "lone genius." For example, Procter & Gamble's *Crest Whitestrips* teeth whitener was created by 3 different divisions: people from the oral care division provided the knowledge for teeth whitening; people from the home care division provided the whitening liquid and people from research and development provided the technology for the strips that stick on teeth to whiten them.

Since team collaboration makes innovation possible, at Procter & Gamble has created more than 20 work communities –a total of 8,000 employees– to solve problems in different areas (perfumes, skin creams, chemicals, detergents, packaging, etc.) and a site called *"Ask me"* where employees can submit problems and questions sent to people with experience on the subject. Procter's former CEO, A.G. Lafley, said, "What most distinguishes this group of men and women is their ability to work *collaboratively*."[219]

The *T-Shape* people concept

In Silicon Valley, companies that innovate seek to hire T-Shape people –where the T's *vertical* line refers to the degree of *depth* that a person has in some discipline (computing, graphic design, economics, etc.) and the *horizontal* line of the T refers to their empathy (the ability to put themselves in the client's shoes and identify with their perspective) and positive attitude to work in multidisciplinary teams. Tim Brown, CEO of IDEO, says they do not want people who have great knowledge in an area yet lack empathy and the ability to work as a team.[220] How does one identify candidates who know how to work as a team?

During interviews, candidates are observed to see whether they talk only about themselves and their achievements or talk about how others have helped them to achieve something. In this second case, there is evidence of empathy, collaboration and interest in working with other people. In addition, IDEO has many internships during which they see how candidates work before hiring them. To promote them, they look at whether they have developed collaboration, whether others seek them out to join their team, or whether they publish and share their knowledge on IDEO's blogs. Brown says that Nike, Procter and Apple also employ the *T-Shape* notion although not as explicitly as IDEO.

In short, innovation is teamwork based on *collaboration*. This does not mean denying the extraordinary value of individual genius but rather highlighting the fact that no one, no matter how brilliant, achieves everything by themselves or possesses all the knowledge. Following this perspective, Sutton says that the people you must try to have in an innovative team are those who show to be creative and intelligent but who also i) are not selfish, ii) share their ideas with others or use the ideas of others while recognizing their merit and iii) help other people succeed.[221]

The job of a good innovation leader is therefore to put together a team following these premises and not look for the solitary genius inside or outside the company. What is more, if in a team there is a lone genius or a person with high individual performance but who *undermines the team's energy by not being collaborative enough*, the team will not perform at its best. This is one of the things that a leader must monitor. As we shall see, a single negative member can reduce the performance of a team by 30% to 40%.

Obstacles to collaboration

Some attitudes conspire against collaboration and hinder innovation. Bosses may preach collaboration while not helping each other, which sends a hypocritical or contradictory message to their teams. When bosses do not set a positive example, others cannot be expected to behave differently. Another case is when a division works well as a team but refuses to collaborate or provide help to other divisions. This transmits a message of selfishness and little collaboration which leads to a vicious circle. It may also be that a boss orders teamwork for no valid reason or asks for resources when they are needed for other more urgent work. Finally, there may be employees who use teamwork as an excuse not to fulfill their *personal responsibilities*. This is what happens with those who move through different divisions giving a hand, but *without finishing what has been assigned to them individually,* or those who make up teams without doing their part. These are known as "butterflies", people that flutter through different divisions.

Another case – Sutton points out – is when a company establishes an evaluation system that leads to *dysfunctional* competition, as in the case of General Electric and Microsoft.[222] General Electric, the company founded by Thomas Edison, used to have a system where 10% of the employees (those considered "Cs") were fired, 20% (the "As") got the best bonuses and awards, while the remaining 70% (the "Bs") shared the leftovers. This evaluation system, known as the Gauss curve or bell (the "rank and yank system"), demoralised employees. This has been admitted by many General Electric executives.

With this type of imposed evaluation, people have no incentive to help others. On the contrary, the incentive is to conspire against others, to speak ill of others, withhold help, and adopt other negative attitudes in order to improve one's own score. This system has changed and nowadays the best performers (the "As") are defined as those who not only have high performance but also *help their colleagues and the business to prosper.*

Microsoft had a similar evaluation system known as "stack ranking" that required each unit to classify a certain percentage of employees as i) high performers, ii) good performers, iii) average and iv) poor performers. Many Microsoft employees interviewed by *Vanity Fair* (2012) have cited this evaluation system as the "most destructive process within Microsoft," something that led to an unknown number of employees leaving the company. "If you were on a team of 10 people –says a former employee–, you walked in the first day knowing that, no matter how good everyone was, 2 people were going to get a great review, 7 were going to get mediocre reviews, and 1 was going to get a terrible review."[223]

This makes employees focus on competing against each other instead of competing with other companies. Quality expert W. Edwards Deming despised these evaluation systems because they force bosses to rate employees whose work is of good or high quality as poor. When people receive unfair and negative evaluations they may become resentful, hurt, bitter, with feelings of inferiority or depressed. Many of them become unfit for work for several weeks, unable to understand why they are considered inferior to others.[224]

The silo mentality

Another case that conspires against collaboration is what is known as the *silo mentality*. *Silos* are closed warehouses for storing corn, wheat, etc. located at a certain distance from each other (e.g. silobags). The closed nature of these warehouses is a metaphor that alludes to the extreme independence and lack of collaboration that may exist between different divisions in a company. The silo mentality can arise for several reasons. People may develop an exclusive identification with their division, forging a *culture of isolation*. As people spend time exclusively with people in their division and none at all with those from other divisions, they limit their points of view and reinforce their ideas and beliefs. In other words, they tend to think the same as those in their division.

In the 1990s, evidence of this was found in a study on 120 Hewlett-Packard ("HP") teams.[225] The members of these teams only interacted with people from their division and over time developed a culture of isolation. They preferred to solve their problems internally because they believed that these were only specific to their division. They refused to ask other divisions for help and, as a result, their performance declined. In one case, HP managers in France refused to go to the HP offices in Belgium because, even though the factory in Belgium perfomed better than the one in France, they did not believe that their Belgium colleagues could teach them anything useful, partly because they saw their problems as unique. They were not, though.

Another case of silo mentality is the attitude of *not sharing ideas or knowledge* because "knowledge is power", which means a person believes himself to be more powerful the more he knows about something and the less others know. There are people who refuse to help others because they think, "Why share my knowledge with others if it makes me less powerful and ultimately expendable?" Another cause of isolation may be the *incentive system*. Many companies set up rewards only for the work performed *within* each division. However, this type of incentive causes people to pay attention only to their own division´s goals, refusing to help people *outside* their division or unit. Another cause is arguing and fighting over *who has the right to develop certain products*. At HP they competed for the same opportunities and this led them to refrain from collaborating. When the time came to transfer technology from one division to another, many engineers were reluctant to collaborate in what they perceived as competitive relationships between their division and the division requesting the technology.[226]

Sony is a company that used to have divisions that were proud to compete with each other. Engineers were encouraged to outperform their colleagues. But the development of the *Connect* system, Sony's "MP3" –that was meant to compete with Apple's *iPod*, required the joint work of five different divisions (the Sony Music team in Japan, Sony Music in the United States, Sony Electronics of the United States, etc.). The problem was that each division had their own idea of what had to be done. While the Sony team in the United States wanted to use a hard drive for music, the Sony team in Japan wanted to use the MiniDisc, and so with other differences. Howard Stringer, the CEO of Sony USA, recalled: "What went wrong at Sony? Silos were a big part of it all."[227]

This resulted in the complete failure of *Connect*, a disappointment for the company that had amazed the world in 1979 with its Walkman. In January 2006, Sony publicly apologised to its customers in Europe and Japan and in August 2007 Stringer ended the production of *Connect*. In contrast, a big part of Apple's success was that all divisions worked together to develop the *iPod*. Apple's Jeff Robbin remarked that it was an "incredible team project. There were no boundaries. The software guys, the hardware guys, the firmware guys, everybody worked together. It was a pretty amazing experience."[228]

Incentives for collaboration

Faced with these obstacles, how does one create incentives that encourage cooperation? In the case of *General Electric*, we have seen that to be qualified and compensated as a type "A" employee or boss, it is not only necessary to do the job well but also to help others succeed. Yet there are other incentives that encourage collaboration. Procter and Gamble, for example, do not use any sophisticated methods to compensate their employees. Former CEO A.G. Lafley would warn that "managers who fail to share ideas simply do not get promoted."[229] At Corning, scientists are able to obtain the title of *Fellow*, which implies retiring in the company and having their own research laboratory, too. For this, they are assessed according to three criteria: i) their colleagues' opinions, ii) being the author of a patent that has generated 100 million dollars and iii) being a secondary author of a colleague's patent, that is, having collaborated in a patent generated by someone else.[230]

One of the most common problems that companies have is designing an economic incentive that encourages collaboration. Many companies preach collaboration but when it comes to rewarding or paying bonuses and prizes they take into account individual performance only. In other words, they send their employees a contradictory message: "cooperate and help whoever needs it but... we will only pay you for your individual tasks." This kind of perverse or poorly designed incentive is common in other areas. For example, in college basketball in the United States, players who pass the ball to their teammates will not accumulate individual points and will have fewer chances of getting hired by a professional NBA team. Therefore, it is more rational for these players to think about themselves first, that is, try to put the ball into the basket themselves, rather than pass it to a teammate.[231]

One must be careful about setting incentives for exclusively individual objectives since people will not have the incentive to collaborate or work well as a team. To avoid this type of contradictory incentive, consulting firm Bain & Company structures each partner's bonus 50% based on individual performance and the other 50% based on proven collaborations.[232] To put it into effect, care is taken to gather all the data on collaboration so that each partner can be assessed in various aspects. In summary, to encourage teamwork it is best to set an economic incentive that takes into account a balance between individual and collaborative tasks.

A mix of novices and experts

As we have seen, innovation is based on teamwork. Now, how is a creative team put together? What type of people should be in it? How many members should it have? The ideal is to combine *experts* and *novices* and have them work together. Experts know what can and cannot be done, which is great in most cases. However, we should note that all knowledge is provisional by nature. It is always subject to subsequent refutations, corrections and new discoveries, says science philosopher Karl Popper (1902-1994). The problem is that many experts assume that they know everything and that there is nothing more to discover. They have firm, immovable opinions: they are not good at changing their points of view or having different perspectives.

On the other hand, novices —precisely because they do not know what can or cannot be done— can provide different perspectives, free from the limitations and customs inherent to every industry or branch of knowledge. An example of this technique of combining novices and experts is that of Jane Goodall and Louis Leakey, a famous English anthropologist. Leakey believed that the study of chimpanzees could provide knowledge for the study of early humans, so he looked for a researcher to conduct observations in the jungle. In 1960 he hired Goodall and sent her to Africa for two years to make observations.

Goodall was a novice in the study of animals; she had no academic knowledge or university degree. She was a 26-year-old English girl who made a living from a white-collar job but loved animals and Tarzan novels. At first, Goodall was hesitant to take the job because she had no college knowledge. But Leakey told her that this knowledge was not necessary since he needed someone "with a mind uncluttered and unbiased by theory who would make the study for no other reason than a real desire for knowledge."[233] She remembers that he wanted someone with an open mind and "not conditioned by previous theories" who would do the study simply out of the desire to learn.[234]

They both realised that if she had not been so ignorant of the existing theories, she would never have been able to observe and explain so many things about chimpanzee behavior. Shortly afterwards, thanks to the research done in Africa, and with Leakey's help, she managed to be accepted at Cambridge University to do a doctorate in ethology, the branch of biology that studies animal behaviour, which she completed in 1965. Goodall is not the only novice who ended up revolutionizing a science through a 'naïve look.'

At the beginning of the 20th century, a young German physicist wrote 4 papers that changed the paradigm of physics. He was only 26 years old. His name is Albert Einstein. People who change scientific paradigms are young or new to the science whose paradigm they change, explains philosopher of science Thomas Kuhn. Unconditioned by the previous rules of that science, they are more likely to see the ones that no longer work.[235] Also young were those who revolutionized the software industry: Steve Jobs started Apple at the age of 21 and Bill Gates founded Microsoft at the age of 20. This also happened in the world of social networks: Mark Zuckerberg created Facebook when he was 20 years old.

The contribution of newbies also occurs with popular products such as the Sony PlayStation. The engineers who developed this console were new to the video game industry. Shigeo Maruyama (Sony) remembers that they were lucky to be amateurs: "We were not preoccupied with established industry practices...we started from square one and let the ideas flow freely and without reservation."[236] Sometimes newbies find the right path thanks to the advice from experts. Such is the case of Larry Page who left university to found Google. Page says that his professor Terry Winograd gave him the "best advice" of his life.[237] He refers to the advice to investigate, in his university thesis, the algorithm that led him to create the Google search engine.

Novices' contributions also appear in industrial processes. Historian Elting Morrison explains that, in the 19th century, ten American steel companies adopted the Bessemer process. As it was an invention used in England, most of these companies imported experienced English workers, except Cambria. At first they all did well, except Cambria, which had no English experts. However, over time it was this company that ended up dominating the American market. This success, says Cambria's president, was due in part to the fact that "We started the converter plant without a single man who had seen even the outside of a Bessemer plant. We thus had willing pupils with no prejudices and no reminiscenses of what they had done in the old country" (England).[238]

Combining delivery and creative skills

Another variant for building teams is to combine some people with creative skills and some with delivery skills. Mark Zuckerberg, Facebook's creative, hired Sheryl Sandberg as Facebook's chief operating officer in 2008 to apply her delivery skills. Sandberg was a brilliant Harvard-educated executive who had worked for Google and as chief of staff for US Treasury Secretary Lawrence Summers. Zuckerberg is grateful that Sandberg "handles the things I don't want to handle," such as advertising strategy, hiring, firing and political issues. "All those things that I would have to do, she does better."[239]

Upon arriving at Facebook (2008), Sandberg's biggest concern was financial: "There was an important question: could we ever make money?" One of the obstacles was that people considered their Facebook pages private and did not want to see them invaded with commercial ads when chatting with friends. However, these ads are what generate income. Facebook had been losing money until Sandberg arrived, but by 2010, it was already a very profitable company. In three years, it grew from 130 employees to 2,500 and from 70 million to almost 700 million users. Creative skills are important for the creation of innovative products, but delivery skills are just as important since they make them profitable and turn them into money.

The founders of Google (Larry Page and Sergey Brin) hired Eric Schmidt (CEO) in 2001, an executive who had previously worked for AT&T, Xerox, Novell and Sun Microsystems. Schmidt was given the task of putting together the corporate infrastructure needed to sustain Google's rapid growth and ensure that quality remained high.[240] Pierre Omidyar, the founder of eBay, clearly knew that his strength was creativity and his weakness was execution. Needing more delivery skills, he hired Jeff Skoll, a Stanford MBA, to run eBay. Omidyar remarked,

> Jeff and I had very complementary skills... He was the one who listen to an idea of mine and says *Ok, let's figure how to get this done.*[241]

The authors of *The Innovator's DNA* say that an innovation team needs creativity to generate novel ideas but also executive work to implement them. Good leaders know this and think carefully about the composition of the team, ensuring that there is sufficient balance between creative and delivery skills. Sometimes creative skills outweigh delivery skills; for example, when creating a product or thinking about the marketing strategy. Other times delivery skills matter more, such as in finance or manufacturing teams. The ideal is to know who has the different skills and to combine them in complementary ways, as Zuckerberg did when he hired Sandberg in 2008.

In addition to this complementarity, innovation requires *multidisciplinary* teams, that is, people with different professions and trades. IDEO, a company dedicated to designing products for different industries, usually assembles multidisciplinary teams that cover three areas: i) the *human factor*, to determine if an innovative idea is "desirable"; ii) the *technical factor*, to determine if an idea is technically possible and iii) the *business factor*, to determine if the idea is economically viable and can make money. For the human factor in their teams, IDEO includes people with knowledge in social sciences, such as anthropologists and psychologists.[242]

For example, if a service is to be designed for people who use wheelchairs, *human factor* people will make sure to spend a day using wheelchairs to understand a person's point of view in this situation. On the other hand, the *technical factor* people are more likely engineers and mechanics who ensure that the chair works properly, for which they will study how its brakes and wheels work, the materials with which it must be built, its resistance, weight, etc. Finally, the people in the *business factor* are those with professions like accountants, specialists in finance, marketing and business administrators who analyse the economic viability of the idea, the funds to finance it, the costs, the profit potential and the sales and advertising channels: *the road to market*.

By putting teams with people from different but complementary professions, IDEO allows for analyzing services and products from several different angles. It is therefore not surprising that it has produced so many innovations. Apple and Disney also use cross-functional teams.[243] As said above, the team that designed the Mac was made up of musicians, poets, artists, zoologists and historians who were also the best computer scientists in the world. The same goes for *Disney Imagineers* whose members include cartoonists, filmmakers, engineers, software imaging specialists, costume designers, architects, and people with mechanical and electrical expertise. This made it possible to design the *Pirates of the Caribbean* animated dummies and other mechanical attractions. In short, innovative companies assemble their teams not only with a mix of people who have creative and delivery skills but also from different professions and trades in order to look at problems from multiple perspectives.

The ideal number of members in a team

Innovative companies usually form small teams. Amazon uses the 'Two Pizza Team' philosophy, meaning the team must be small enough to feed on two pizzas, from 6 to 10 people. With many small teams, Amazon can work on a large number of projects and thus test different product or service models. Likewise, Google engineers work in teams of 3 to 6 people. Google tries to keep teams small because "there is not much productivity in large groups."[244] The result is a flexible organization with teams working on hundreds of projects, a strategy Schmidt calls "letting a thousand flowers bloom.", borrowing Mao´s words. With hundreds of small teams developing ideas, it is not surprising that Google comes up with so many novel products. The authors of *The Innovator's DNA* say that many companies fail when trying to innovate because they do not understand a basic organisational principle: the more radical the innovation, the more *autonomy* the team must have in respect of the rest of the company structure.

Apple purposely tries to act as if it were still a startup, putting small teams on crucial projects. For example, only 2 engineers wrote the Safari browser code for the *iPad* –a challenging project.[245] In a 2010 interview, Jobs argued that Apple is a company that does not have all the resources. "And the way we've been successful is by choosing very carefully which horses to ride." At first glance this statement seems absurd because Apple had about $200 billion in cash and investments –according to February 2022 estimates.[246] However, Apple's beginnings in the 1970s were difficult and from that time the custom remained to act *as if resources were scarce*. We have always "fought for resources" says an Apple executive. "Steve and Tim in general want to be sure you need what you're asking for."[247]

Bill Campbell (1940-2016) was a famous Silicon Valley executive, known for mentoring many innovators such as Larry Page and Steve Jobs, among others. Not only was he on the board of directors of Apple —a company he helped survive when it was on the verge of bankruptcy in 1997— but for many years he would go for walks on Sundays with Jobs (they lived in the same neighbourhood) for a couple of hours to discuss Jobs' management style and personal problems. In a talk Campbell gave before he died, he told a group of executives in Silicon Valley, "most of you have boards that are too big" and described how on Apple's board there are only 7 people but they don't spend much time meeting because they are usually divided into subgroups.[248]

One of the problems in large companies is that they assemble large teams due to the excitement of being big and the political power that this implies. If an executive has a large team it tends to show that "he is very important." Researcher J. Richard Hackman (Harvard) has spent almost 50 years studying teams of all kinds: airline pilots, doctors, product development teams, symphony orchestras, military commands, etc.[249] The ideal number, Hackman concludes, is 4 to 6 members and in no case should a team have more than 10 members because, as the team size increases, organizational and performance problems grow "exponentially", e.g. arguments increase about who is the boss or who is in charge of which task.

James H. Webb, a Marine, says combat units were reduced from 12 members to 4 during World War II. Webb says groups of 12 were "immensely difficult" for leaders to control, especially in the stressful and confusing situations that wars create. Solving coordination problems and creating friendly relationships that lead soldiers to "give their life for their companion or friend" were more difficult in groups of 12.

Navy Seals teams also understand that 4 is the optimal number for combat. Consulting firm McKinsey's teams are made up of 3 members and a manager. Brad Smith, CEO of Intuit —a successful software company— says that development teams cannot be larger than the number of people fed by two pizzas, because this helps them remain agile and reach decisions quickly. This lesson also applies to small organizations like the team that developed the *Pulse News* app, created for the *iPad* by two Stanford students, Akshay Kothari and Ankit Gupta. These inventors say that once they had divided their staff of 8 into three teams, they produced better software, faster, and with less talking or arguing.[250]

These findings and experiences explain why the average restaurant reservation in the United States is for 4 people. Think of the last time you had dinner with a group of 10 or 15 people. It is difficult –perhaps impossible– to have a coherent and satisfying conversation that involves the entire group. Generally, the group is divided into subgroups or pairs. One of the first things Sutton asks when he goes to a company with conflicts is "How many members does your team have?" If the answer is more than 5 or 6 members, especially more than 10, his advice is to remove some members or divide them into subgroups, which has shown good results.

In terms of stability, some think that it is always good to bring new people into a team. But even if you bring talented people on board, it takes time for them to learn to work well with others, to get to know their strengths and weaknesses. In general, the longer they work together, the more effective they will be. For example, in surgical teams (surgeons, anesthesiologists and nurses) there is evidence that the longer they work together, the lower the error and mortality rate.[251] The same goes for airplane pilots and co-pilots: in 1994, the *United States National Transportation Safety Board* found that 73% of errors on commercial airplanes occurred in the first 24 hours that a team worked together, side by side.[252] This Board also found that 44% of these errors took place during *the team's first flight*.

A study of 98 semiconductor companies founded in the United States from 1978 to 1985 found that when teams of founding members had worked together elsewhere before, their companies were more financially successful in the first two years, a success that continued to improve in the following years.[253] Finally, teams also need "new blood" to generate different ideas. There comes a time when they become obsolete, that is, productivity and creativity decrease over the years. A study on research and development teams discovered that their members are productive during the first four years and that their productivity begins to decrease after about five years.[254] Therefore, "new blood" is recommended for teams with more than five years with the same members.

Negativism in the team

One of the most serious problems that a team can have is having members who are negative, problematic or downright bad people, an issue known as having "bad apples" in the basket. Innovation requires a positive spirit, trusting that the impossible is possible. It is difficult to achieve. Therefore, anyone who is negative or problematic can destroy the work environment. According to a series of studies summarised by Will Felps and his colleagues, one "bad apple" in a small group— that is, someone who is unpleasant, negative, lazy, selfish, rude, or incompetent— can reduce team performance by 30% to 40 percent, compared to teams that are free from this kind of members.[255]

There are three reasons why these people reduce performance. The first is that they *pass on their negativity onto other members*, that is, others end up copying their bad attitudes. Seeing somebody acting antisocially makes other members feel *less inhibited from behaving in the same way*. In an experiment that Felps conducted with a small group, he observed that "when someone acted like an idiot," the other members began to copy that person's attitudes. There is an imitation or *spillover effect*. The member who is a "bad apple" ends up rotting the other "apples" in the basket.

The second is that people end up spending more time dealing with the negative member, commenting on what that member does or says, and *less time doing their jobs*. Studies indicate that the feelings of anxiety, anger or sadness generated by negative members end up distracting and demotivating the team. To protect themselves from these negative attitudes, some members may try to pay no attention and seek positive experiences such as going out for lunch, having a few drinks (happy hour) or surfing the Internet, but all of this ends up turning into factors that distract and affect the team's performance.

The third reason is that negativity *reduces team creativity*. According to studies, teams made up of emotionally unstable members have *fewer ideas than those with stable, calm members*. Teams with two problematic members and two stable members have less creativity too. There are also studies that state that *positive feelings facilitate creativity*. This depends on several conditions, such as free exchange of ideas, confidence that innovation is possible and enthusiasm to create something new, all of which are difficult in negative environments.

Therefore, a situation where someone teases or makes harsh comments leads people to feel inhibited, act defensively or remain silent, which reduces creativity. In short, the problem with negativity is that it has a multiplying effect, that is, an effect of contagion, imitation, distraction and inhibition of productivity and creativity, even if it starts with a single person. Human beings are generally guided and behave according to the example closest to them. Therefore people with a positive and respectful attitude towards team members are essential.

Now, the hallmark of good leaders is that when there is a problematic or negative member, they call them to order: they warn them to change their attitude. They do not let their bad behaviour contaminate the rest of the team. This is essential so that the other members feel protected, psychologically safe. Eventually, the leader may consider removing that member from the team or even firing him or her from the company if the warnings have no effect. One of Fortune's "100 Best Companies to Work For" in 2008 was Baird (No. 39), a financial company in western United States. Paul Purcell, its CEO, says his rule is "don't put up with assholes." To enforce it, Purcell tells people in interviews: "If I discover that you are an asshole, I am going to fire you." What is an asshole? For Purcell it is being someone who constantly puts his or her own needs before his or her colleagues' and clients'.[256] This warning seems to work because Baird climbed from 39 place to 11th place on Fortune's list (2010) of the best companies to work for due to its positive environment.

However, it should be noted that someone with a problematic character can be transformed or turned into someone better if they are guided and led to understand what they are doing wrong through a temporary tutor. Sutton recalled there was an executive who was technically very capable but personally negative. Then he was told, "We are going to put you in charge of the next project, but if you act like you did in the last one we will fire you. However, if you succeed, we will give you a big bonus."[257] The CEO supervised this project and trained him personally and thus turned this worker, who was technically good but had a bad character, into someone much more pleasant. An alternative is to give them *coaching* sessions, a service increasingly used by companies given the importance that good personal relationships have for business success.

The bad is stronger than the good

All of this is reinforced by a major academic study called "Bad is Stronger than Good" by Kathleen D. Vohs and colleagues, which reviewed all the existing evidence on the effect that bad has. They found that people have more vivid memories of "bad emotions, bad parents, and bad feedback."[258] People tend to think about these issues more than about positive emotions. This study reports several experiments. In one of these, 17,000 research articles published in psychology journals were evaluated and it revealed that *negative topics exceed positive topics by a ratio of 69% to 31%*. Another experiment showed that the euphoria of winning the lottery does not last long and that the winner's level of happiness or unhappiness quickly returns to what it was before winning the lottery. Therefore, if they were negative or bitter, they become so again despite having become millionaires. Another study found that the experience of bad sex far outweighs the benefits of good sex. In another study, several people were asked to remember recent events in their lives with emotional impact and they reported negative events much more than positive ones. It was also found that people remember bosses or colleagues who blocked or stopped them from achieving their goals much more than those who helped them.

In journalism, bad news are considered to attract more than good news and sell more newspapers. Interviews with children and adults up to 50 years of age revealed that negative memories from childhood have much more weight than positive ones, even in the case of people who have had a relatively happy childhood.[259] To be classified as a bad person, some negative acts are enough while positive acts have less weight. In a study of 238 cancer patients, 70 died: The optimism of some patients did not predict their death, but *pessimism had a high rate of predicting mortality*.

Finally, something useful not only for work, but for life as in a couple, is a group of studies that discovered the 5 to 1 rule for romantic relationships, courtships and marriages.[260] This rule states that for every bad interaction with your partner, at least *five good interactions are needed to compensate or repair i*t. Otherwise, the relationship is destined to fail. The frequency, intensity, and reciprocity of negative interactions are more predictive of divorce than positive interactions.

This same rule applies to interactions with bosses and coworkers. On average, negative interactions (such as loud arguments, with insults or sarcasm) are *five times more powerful than positive ones*. Therefore, it is crucial that leaders take care to warn or sanction problematic members. If they do not, the negativity ends up affecting the entire team. In short, whether for routine work or (even more so) for creativity, eliminating the negative is more important than highlighting the positive.

> Whether you think you can, or you think you can´t, you are right.[261]
>
> Henry Ford

Chapter 6

Believe in the impossible

Once a team is formed, work begins. With what spirit? With great optimism, the trait of innovators. Here are some examples. Elon Musk says: "We specialize in making the imposible.."[262] Another example is Brad Bird (Pixar), Oscar winner for *The Incredibles* and *Ratatouille*. He explains, "The first step in achieving the impossible is believing that the impossible can be achieved", likewise, Walt Disney said, "It´s kinf of fun to do the impossible."[263] As we see, innovators believe that they can do fantastic things. But the first step is to *believe*. An innovation team needs people who begin to work believing that big dreams can be achieved, no matter how many obstacles and difficulties may arise.

Faith is important in that it reduces the rate of failure through the *self-fulfilling prophecy* 'If you think you can, you can. If you think you can't, you can't.' The point is that if a team believes it can achieve great things, it will tend to be more persevering and energetic. There have been more than 500 studies on this self-fulfilling prophecy. They show that giving people confidence makes them do better. When the leader believes in his team and has positive expectations, the team ends up doing better.[264]

Dov Eden and Abraham Shani (professors at Tel Aviv University), conducted one of the most interesting studies on this self-fulfilling prophecy in an Israeli army military camp.[265] At the beginning of the training, the instructors were given a list with some names of soldiers and were told that they had "exceptional potential" and would do very well in the training. However, this was not true since, objectively, they had no such potential. No other information was given to the instructors (they were deceived by those who set up the experiment). Nor did the soldiers know that they were the subject of a study.

What is more, they were randomly assigned – mingled – into different teams with the rest. Well, the soldiers with "exceptional potential" did much better than the rest, approximately 50% better than their peers in all tasks: navigation manoeuvres, firing weapons, combat tactics, etc. Why? Their instructors had given them confidence that they would be the best and gave them all the resources and attention: they led them to believe in themselves. The instructors acted as paternal figures, like "fathers" transmitting confidence and self-esteem to their "children." Trust transmitted by a leader to their team is therefore decisive for innovation, something that is difficult to achieve.

The role of critical members

People with a critical sense can also be useful for innovation: some studies state that "faultfinders" are better at detecting flaws and errors in projects and ideas. In the bank loans area, for example, some critical people are better at writing off bad loans and help to avoid losing money. This type of personality can compensate for the extreme optimism of some dreamer-entrepreneurs who believe that their projects will succeed, no matter how unrealistic they may be. Some pharmaceutical companies offer large sums of money (e.g. $20,000) to managers who cancel their own research and development projects as an incentive for cancelling on time.

Because some projects require investing billions of dollars, yet some managers continue running them even after realising they are doomed.[266] They are reluctant to admit being responsible for a failure that could cost the company billions. A Stanford study found that MBA students and engineers with critical personalities were good at finding negative facts and took fewer risks when deciding whether to drive a car with a bad engine.[267] Their decision had elements of realism, especially considering that these students and engineers analysed real data from the failure of the NASA Challenger engine that exploded in 1986. Ultimately, it can be worthwhile having a critical person in a team, acting as a counterweight to those who are excessively idealistic.

"Optimistic but concerned" members

According to studies by Christina Fong (University of Washington, Seattle), "emotionally ambivalent" people are more creative than those who are fully optimistic or fully pessimistic. The ambivalent are more like the "happy but worried" people who are always optimistic about the long term *but also worry about every little detail*. David Kelly, founder of IDEO, is the classic example of someone who is optimistic about the long term but always worries about the details. This is the ideal attitude of an innovative leader. Managers must recognise that emotional ambivalence can have "positive consequences for the success of the organization." In one of these studies, they asked 102 college students to write about certain emotional experiences in their lives in order to evoke in them feelings of happiness, sadness, ambivalence, or neutrality.

He then had them complete a creativity test called the *Remote Associates Test* that explored their ability to recognise common themes between seemingly unrelated words. The results showed that there were no differences between happy, sad and neutral individuals. In contrast, "emotionally ambivalent" people performed much better on this creativity task. When people have mixed or ambivalent emotions, they interpret them as signs of a situation that may have many *unusual associations* and will need responding with more creative thinking.

"Managers who want to increase the creative output of their employees," Fong concludes, "might benefit from following in the footsteps of companies like design firm IDEO or Walt Disney, which pride themselves on maintaining odd working environments. On some level, the bicycles that hang from the ceiling at IDEO and the colorful, casual environment at Disney probably help their employees sharpen their abilities to come up with novel and innovative ideas."[268]

However, if we return to the notion that "the bad is stronger than the good", the problem with pessimists or negative people is that they spread their bad mood onto their colleagues. Studies show that a bad mood can spread to the entire company or team.[269] When faced with such a member, as we have seen, it is advisable to stop their attitude in time, to remove them from the team – or isolate them, as one company did.

There was an engineer –says Sutton– who was admired for his ability to detect failures and errors but at the same time, he was feared and despised for being a "100 percent bad person."[270] On every occasion, no matter what type of project it was, he not only destroyed the ideas of his colleagues but also humiliated them personally. However, as he was very good at his job, his bosses refused to fire him. He was then moved to a private office in a building away from the team. In this way, his colleagues and bosses managed to have minimal contact with him.

Does money encourage creativity?

Money has a huge effect on how people strive. It influences the jobs they choose, who they marry, etc. Many economists believe that paying good salaries is enough to make people work harder and better, to increase their productivity. However, some problems must be considered when using money as an incentive for creativity. A certain company, says Sutton, decided to use the money as a stimulus. The idea was to offer a financial reward to people who proposed good ideas. Then management said, "every time we have a brainstorming session, to make it productive, we will pay people for their good ideas." What they did was count each person's ideas and give them $7 per idea.[271] It was a team of eight engineers. So if someone had five good ideas he could take home $35 at the end of the meeting. What was the outcome?

All kinds of problems arose, such as arguments about "whose idea was it?", "did someone copy mine using other words?" and so on. First, when engineers went to these brainstorming meetings, they stopped talking to each other and expressing their good ideas *for fear that someone else would copy them*. Then, at the end of each meeting, they began arguing over who *should keep the $7 per idea*. Finally, instead of everyone collaborating to have good ideas, *the number of ideas decreased*. Management had hoped to increase the number of ideas but because of this dysfunctional competition they obtained the opposite effect: fewer ideas. This is a classic case of a poorly designed financial incentive; even though it is meant to foster collaboration between team members, it only rewards *individual* work. Money can then inhibit creativity, which, as we have seen, requires collaboration and a positive environment.

Kathleen Vohs and colleagues conducted a series of experiments to study the influence of money on people's minds. In one experiment, they sat a group of participants at a table to play *Monopoly* with fake money.[272] After a few minutes, the board game was taken off the table leaving some of them with USD 4000 in cash and others with USD 200. After a while one of the experimenters went in with a tray of pencils and intentionally let it fall on the floor. He did it "by accident" in order to see who would help him pick up the pencils from the floor. Well, those who had USD 4,000 helped much less in collecting pencils than those who had only USD 200.

Another part of the experiment showed that when they were given the option of doing group or individual work, they chose to work alone and even sit further away from each other. Although the people in these experiments did not realise they were being manipulated with money, its mere presence led them to be less cooperative. The moral is that focusing on the money and not on the task at hand can create dysfunctional competition and an environment of poor collaboration.

Money can also condition objectives. At Apple only one person, the CFO, is responsible for dealing with expenses and this is partly because Steve Jobs believed that it was not a good thing for people to think about money because it inhibits the pursuit of excellence. As we have seen, one of the questions Jobs asked his team – in the 1990s, when Apple had budget restrictions – was, "What would you do if money were no object?"[273] By removing this restriction, they focused on achieving what Apple customers wanted, regardless of the cost.

Cartoonist and businessman Walt Disney's mantra was "I don't make movies to make money—I make money to make movies." Brad Bird says: "It seems counterintuitive, but for imagination-based companies to succeed in the long run, making money can't be the focus."[274] In short, money is a very important motivator, and it is undoubtedly the reason why many people join companies like Apple, Disney or Google, where there are opportunities to make a lot of money. There is nothing wrong with that. However, using money in certain ways can inhibit collaboration and creativity, which are essential for innovation.

Money and the passion to innovate

To innovate, it is important to hire people who like the type of work done in the company and not those who just do it for the money. A consultant who worked for Apple said that people come in and stay because they believe in the mission of this company. Many of its employees had been dreaming of working at Apple since they were children, when they acquired their first Mac computer. "At Apple you work on Apple products. If you're a diehard Apple geek, it's magical," says Andrew Borovsky, a former employee.[275] The formula of doing something you are passionate about is the one used by great innovators and in general by all those who achieve great things in life. Steve Jobs was passionate about his work. He wanted to make money but that was not his only motivation. He had the ability to transmit that passion to his teams. This is how he explained it in a memorable speech to Stanford students in 2005:

> I'm convinced that the only thing that kept me going [after being fired from Apple in 1985] was that I loved what I did. You've got to find what you love. And that is as true for your work as it is for your lovers. Your work is going to fill a large part of your life, and the only way to be truly satisfied is to do what you believe is great work. And the only way to do great work is to love what you do. If you haven't found it yet, keep looking. Don't settle (...) Don't let the noise of others' opinions drown out your own inner voice. And most important, have the courage to follow your heart and intuition. They somehow already know what you truly want to become. Everything else is secondary.[276]

Djokovic and Nadal continue playing tennis as if they were just starting their careers, despite being veterans and the millions of dollars they have in the bank. A former coach of Federer recalls, "Roger still finds happiness in hitting the ball, going to the gym, travelling... He just loves playing tennis."[277] (Federer retired in 2022). Passion is also part of the concept of vocation or *calling*. Some people have a vocation for what they do. They feel that they could not do anything else, whether they be doctors, architects, psychologists, teachers, accountants, lawyers or entrepreneurs. They like what they do, their work is their main retribution, while money is secondary, the result of what they do. Vocation also explains why money is far from being the main incentive in professions and trades such as those of priests, soldiers, teachers, social workers, and so on.

Motivation or passion is more important than it seems because, according to Gallup polls, more than 50% of employees in the United States do not feel any passion for their work and 20% are totally unmotivated. This has a cost of 300 billion dollars per year in lost productivity. In some countries only 2% to 3% of the workforce feel motivated by their work.[278]

Autonomy fosters enthusiasm

Many companies are discovering that one of the characteristics that leads to having passionate employees is what they call "autonomy". It consists of four aspects: what people do, when they do it, how they do it, and who they do it with. A good step is to allow workers to choose the task they prefer to do, as far as possible. It is obvious that if a person is forced to do something they do not like, we can hardly expect to see passion or enthusiasm. It is also advisable to let people choose who to work with or what team to join. At Facebook, new engineers spend 6 months in training, fixing software viruses, learning the company culture and getting to know their colleagues. After having interviewed several teams, they decide which one they want to join. In W. L. Gore & Associates, makers of the durable GORE-TEX fabric, anyone looking to move up in the company and lead a team has to have people who want to work with them.[279]

Letting them choose their resting time is also advisable. Netflix has an unusual vacation policy. Employees can take as many vacation days as they want as long as their work is covered. Managers and employees do not keep track of how many days each person takes. The company policy is: "We should focus on what people get done, not how many hours or days worked."[280] All this makes "autonomy" one of the characteristics for passion to emerge. Daniel Pink commented on several examples of "autonomy." The first was the case of Atlassian, an Australian software company named after the Greek titan Atlas who carried the world on his shoulders. In 2002, Scott Farquhar and Mike Cannon-Brookes, two Australians who had just graduated from university, took out $10,000 on their credit cards to start a software company.

The goal was to compete with large companies. At the time, it seemed utopian, but today Atlassian has net profits of more than $100 million a year and employs 3,000 people in offices in seven countries. Cannon-Brookes had seen successful businesses stagnate and wanted to avoid that fate for his own. Therefore, to boost his team's enthusiasm and creativity, he decided to give them permission to spend a day *working on any software improvement or development they wanted*, even if it was not part of their regular work. This day of experimentation has given rise to several new products and also improvements on existing ones. This day of creativity and autonomy (once a quarter) begins on Thursdays at two in the afternoon. Many work during the night. Then, at four in the afternoon on Fridays, they show the results to the rest of the company in a meeting over cold beer and chocolate cake.

Atlassian calls these bursts of creativity "FedEx Days," as people have 24 hours to deliver their product (in reference to the Federal Express company). Over the years, this experiment has produced some of the company's most innovative software. In terms of money, Cannon-Brookes believes that "if you don't pay enough, you can lose people. But beyond that, money is not a motivator. What matters are these other features."[281] These characteristics are "autonomy", that is, allowing your engineers to decide *what to work on and who to work with*. Seeing the positive results that the FedEx day generated, he decided to give 20% free time per month for engineers to work on a task of their choice.

In another example, Professor Teresa Amabile (Harvard) and her team studied 23 professional artists who had been hired to make paintings, some of them on commission – for money – and others without commission, that is, not for money, just for passion. Amabile handed the works they painted to a panel of artists and curators to assess the paintings for creativity and technical skill. The results were surprising. The commissioned works –in exchange for money– were rated as significantly less creative than the works that had not been commissioned (no money). One of the artists reported that he felt more limited when he did work for money than when he did work for pleasure or passion:

Not always, but a lot of the time, when you are doing a piece for someone else it becomes more "work" than joy. When I work for myself ther is the pure joy of creating and I can work through the night and not even know it. On a commissioned piece you have to check yourself–be careful to do what the client wants.[282]

Some studies show that financial rewards are effective when the task is simple and repetitive, such as working on an assembly line in a factory.[283] Not so when it comes to creative work, such as painting pictures or composing music. That is, in simple and repetitive (boring) tasks, paying a better salary makes people increase their productivity. But in creative tasks it does not lead to higher but lower performance, as was found in this study of 23 artists.

The case of the MSN Encarta encyclopedia (Microsoft)

Some innovations were born driven by passion rather than by the desire to make money. Pink says,

> Imagine it's 1996. You sit down with an economist–an accomplished business school professor with a Ph. D. in economics. You say to her: "I've got a crystal ball here that ca peer fifteen years into the future. I'd like to test your forecasting powers (...) I'm going to describe two new encyclopedias– one just out, the other to be launched in a few years. You have to predict which will be more successful in 2011.
>
> The first encyclopedia will be made by Microsoft. As you know, Microsoft is a large and successful company. Moreover, with the introduction of Windows 95, it is about to become a global software colossus. Microsoft will finance this encyclopedia: it will pay professional writers and editors to make articles on thousands of topics. Microsoft managers will oversee the project to ensure it is

completed on time. Microsoft will then sell the encyclopaedia on CD-ROMs online.

On the other hand, the second innovation will not come from a company but will be designed by tens of thousands of people writing and editing articles just for fun, autonomously. These fans will not need any special qualifications to participate. The most important thing is that *no one will be paid a single dollar*. These people will have to do their jobs without anyone supervising them and without anyone paying them, sometimes working up to twenty or thirty hours a week, for free! This encyclopedia, which will exist online, will also be free for users, anyone will be able to use it. Then you ask the economics professor, "In 2011, one of these two will be the largest and most popular in the world and the other will be a failure. Which one is which?"

'In 1996', continues Pink, 'I doubt you could have found a single sober economist anywhere on planet Earth who would not have picked that first model as the success" [i.e. Microsoft's encyclopedia]. It would have been like asking a zoologist who would win a 200-meter footrace between a cheetah and your brother-in-law". There was no way a product created *free of charge* could compete with Microsoft's model. However, today we know how this story ended. On October 31, 2009, Microsoft pulled the plug on the MSN Encarta encyclopaedia, which had been on the market for sixteen years. In other words, Microsoft's encyclopedia failed, despite all the money and technological resources behind it. Instead, Wikipedia, the model with millions of individuals contributing for free, became the largest and most popular encyclopedia in the world. Just eight years after its creation, Wikipedia had more than 17 million articles in some 270 languages, including 3.5 million in English.[284]

Constructive conflicts

When teams perform creative tasks and struggle in an atmosphere of mutual respect, they have better ideas. Some companies even give employees a course on how to have constructive confrontations. For example, Intel has been using constructive confrontation since its foundation in 1968. All new employees take lessons on how to use it. Intel employees say that sometimes fights get ugly or, on the contrary, overly diplomatic.[285] In the hands of a good leader, these quarrels can produce positive results, especially when people fight as equals for their ideas. To achieve this, it is essential to forbid the use of rank and hierarchies so that no one can tell another to shut up.

Earlier we mentioned Bob Taylor, who led the ARPANET team, the predecessor of the internet. He later worked as manager for Xerox Parc, the laboratory where many of today's innovations were created: the Alto personal computer (1972), the word processor, the mouse, the graphics interface, the laser printer, hypertext, Ethernet, and TCP/IP protocols for data transfer. At Xerox Parc, Taylor hosted weekly meetings during which a different speaker each week would propose an idea and try to defend it in the face of questions and criticism from some of the most creative engineers in the world. They were *constructive* confrontations since, as Michael Hiltzik says in his book *Dealers of Lighting Xerox PARC and the Dawn of the Computer Age*, "Impugning a man's thinking was acceptable, but never his character. Taylor strived to create a democracy where everyone's ideas were impartially subject to the group's learned demolition, regardless of the proponent's credentials or rank."[286]

In other words, he wanted there to be criticism and discussions, not to attack but to improve the proposed idea. Each person's position or hierarchy did not matter. Everyone was subjected to the team's opinions and observations. When people fight over ideas, when they argue about which are better, creativity increases, as was the case in the legendary Xerox Parc under Taylor's leadership. On the other hand, when people fight because they despise each other, when there are personal grudges and the exchange of opinions becomes unpleasant, creativity decreases.

Therefore, one of the requirements when leading an innovation team is to create an atmosphere where there is *freedom of expression* and debate –but with respect. Steve Jobs was said to have a reputation for always imposing his ideas, but Ed Catmull, the co-founder of Pixar, thinks differently, "Steve had a remarkable ability to leave behind things that didn't work. If you were in an argument with him, and you convinced him that you were right, he would change his mind quickly. He didn't cling to an idea because he had once thought it was brilliant. His ego didn't stick to the suggestions he made, even when he put his full weight behind them. When Steve saw the Pixar directors do the same, he recognized them as kindred spirits."[287]

Debra Dunn, a former Hewlett-Packard executive, and Robert Sutton advise the following steps for constructive confrontation:[288]

1. Don't allow criticism when generating ideas. Make it comfortable and safe for people to suggest the craziest or most controversial ideas possible. When ideas are being proposed, you should not attack them. It is important to let them flow and you must therefore avoid criticizing them. Once you have some ideas, invite people to criticize or challenge them, if possible by proposing better ideas.

2. Involve everyone in the task. Intervene when some talk too much and encourage those who are silent to speak their minds. Sometimes the most valuable contribution comes from the *most timid and silent ones*.

3. Don't just listen to people's words: observe also their gestures. Are they smiling? Are they paying attention? Do they make disapproving gestures with their eyes or faces? The leader must set an example with *constructive* gesture behaviour and watch out for those who, perhaps without realizing, make negative gestures.

4. Learn each person's peculiarities. Some people may be "thick-skinned" and endure criticism without taking offense, while others may be so sensitive that even the mildest criticism may inhibit or anger them.

5. Once the meeting is over, do some "damage control." Calm down those who feel personally hurt or whose ideas have been harshly criticized. If someone has made personal offensive remarks, call them

and tell them to never do it again. In some cases it may be useful to help them to clearly see the difference between personal attacks (hostility and anger) and disagreements on *what* should be done (objectives, methods, solutions, etc.).

IDEO brainstorming sessions go through three phases. First ideas are put forward during forty or fifty minutes and then the leader says "Right. That's it, now let's discuss these ideas." It is important to know when to fight over an idea and when to keep quiet so that everyone feels comfortable expressing their own ideas, without fear of ridicule or objections (psychological safety). In some of these meetings, it may be advisable for the boss or team leader not to be present, since some people may feel inhibited in their presence. David Kelley (IDEO) makes a habit of quietly leaving the room.[289] That is, he can call a meeting but if things are going well and the conversation is productive, he leaves without attracting attention, because he knows that his *authority figure can create discomfort* and the discussion can be more creative in his absence.

Once a decision has been made, confrontation and discussions must be left behind because these undermine the process of *implementing* ideas. Indeed, there is a point where the teams argue about which path to follow or which idea to implement. But once a decision has been made, *you must help implement it as best as possible even if it is not the idea that you like*. In this regard, Andy Grove, the former CEO of Intel, has a motto for this situation: "First disagree and then compromise." Grove explains:

> If you disagree with an idea, you should work especially hard to implement it well because that way when it fails you'll know it was a bad idea. Not bad execution.[290]

The key is knowing how to accept defeat gracefully and provide all possible collaboration so that no one can say that help was withheld because they did not believe in the idea. It is not easy to do but it is a trait of good innovation teams. Finally, going back to the differences between routine work and innovative work, it is worth clarifying that when there are people doing routine work, quarrels and arguments generally have negative effects. For example, if two pilots flying a plane are arguing about how to land it, it may be a bad sign. The same if two surgeons argue on how to operate on a heart while the patient is lying with his chest open. The confrontations we refer to are those that have room for *trial and error*, as in creative work that consists in having many ideas in order to have better chances of producing a high quality idea.

How to motivate the team. The role of emotions

To motivate a team you need to try to stimulate its members rather than simply present rational arguments. Neuroscientists claim that "we are not rational, but emotional beings who reason", that is, we act driven by what we feel. To support this, they maintain that the pre-frontal cortex brain, where reason is, appeared about 100 thousand years ago, while the limbic brain, where emotions are, is much older: about 200 million years old.[291] Therefore, before reasoning, the human being *felt emotions;* for example, the fear that the first humans felt when faced with the danger of a lurking beast.

The words *motivate* and *excite* come from the Latin *motivus* and *motio*, which mean movement. Emotions lead to action, while reason justifies it. Getting people excited is therefore the secret to *getting the team moving*. In the business world, John Kotter (Harvard) says that changes in companies and teams are achieved once the emotions of individuals are changed. Kotter studied 400 people in 130 organizations and observed that people's behaviour changed *when their emotions were influenced*, not just their rational part.[292]

In spite of this, there is a myth about emotions always being detrimental to logical reasoning. Antonio Damasio, a Portuguese neuroscientist, did research on this.[293] He maintains that since the influence of philosopher René Descartes —the father of rationalism— people started to believe more firmly that correct decisions could only be made with a "cool head" and that emotions and reason should not mix but kept apart like oil and water. There is no doubt that under certain circumstances, emotion disturbs reasoning. Evidence abounds and popular advice reminds us, "Keep a cool head, keep emotions at bay! Don't let your passions interfere with your decisions." However, Damasio's experiments showed that *the lack of emotion is also harmful*. In his work with patients who had suffered emotional brain injuries, he came across a brilliant, intelligent, yet unemotional man.

This individual, whom Damasio called Elliot (his pseudonym), passed all intelligence tests with high scores. In interpersonal relationships he was a pleasant individual, with a respectful and diplomatic composure. The problem was that, when it came to choosing between several alternatives, he could not because he lacked the emotion that would allow him to say *what he liked best*. For example, when he had to decide where to go for dinner he could brilliantly analyse the advantages and disadvantages of all the restaurants, but in the end he remained undecided because he lacked emotion and could not *sense* which one appealed to him most. He himself realised this impediment and told Damasio with a smile, "And after all this, I still didn't know what to do!"[294]

In short, knowing how to manage emotions is essential to reason and decide better. Psychologist Daniel Goleman – author of the bestseller *Emotional Intelligence* – maintains that people who manage to understand and manage their emotions in different life situations, "have an 85% greater chance of being more successful in their jobs and in making important life decisions." Those with great emotional intelligence, respect the feelings of others, use their emotions to make important decisions, assume responsibility for what they feel, distinguish well between what they think and feel, avoid controlling, blaming or judging others, and seek positive results from their negative emotions. They are also happier.[295]

Strategies to motivate

As we know, emotions can be positive but also negative. As to the positive ones, research shows that happiness leads people to be more creative when it comes to solving problems.[296] On the other hand, rejection can create health problems. A study that followed 3,122 men during ten years found that those who had good bosses suffered fewer heart attacks than those with bad bosses.[297] According to studies, the two strongest emotions are anger and pride. Anger or resentment lead to quarrels between couples or families, to wars between nations or tribes, ideological hatred, genocide and murder, revenge and fierce crime. Whereas pride explains why people and companies want to achieve great things to be proud of. Many young people proudly mention the place where they work: "I work for Apple", "I am a manager at Facebook", etc.

Two strategies to incite anger are *naming an enemy* and *naming a problem*, according to professors Robert Sutton and Huggy Rao (Stanford) in *Scalling Up Excellence*. Naming an enemy is a very effective method since *people unite when a common enemy appears*. Steve Jobs used this strategy to motivate his teams and attract his clients' attention. He criticised large companies and especially IBM, which he portrayed as "an evil dictatorship…with its soulless wares."[298]

He said "the only problem with Microsoft is they just have no taste…I don´t mean that in a small way, I mean that in a big way. In the sense that they don´t think of original ideas, and they don´t bring much culture into their products." In his last days before his death, he said that Larry Page (Google) had copied Apple's ideas and had no creativity. When he returned to Apple in 1997 he gave a speech on how he would make it great again and someone in the audience asked him about his competitor Michael Dell and Jobs replied, "Fuck Michael Dell!" Then he said that the stock had plummeted but that he would do a new 3-year bond issue, and finally said, "If you want to make Apple great again, let´s get going. If not, get the hell out." John

Lilly, a former employee who attended the meeting, remarked, "I think it´s not an overstatement to say that just about everyone in the room loved him a that point, would have followed him off a cliff if that´s where he led."[299]

This is a classic example of *naming an enemy* using anger against other competitors but also the *pride* that would come from making Apple a brilliant company again. Of course, this strategy should not lead to indecent or distasteful behaviour, like some British Airways employees did when they covertly called customers of Virgin Atlantic Airways (Richard Branson's company) and lied to them, claiming that Virgin had cancelled their flights and that Branson had AIDS.[300] Another case using anger is the one employed by some British Petroleum executives, according to Professor Rao. When they were enlarging the retail division, which meant expanding the number of gas stations, they adopted the slogan 'Slam the Clam' referring to *Royal Dutch Shell*—whose logo is a *clam*, British Petroleum's main competitor. Almost everything they did at British Petroleum such as establishing locations for new gas stations, allocating more budget, hiring more employees, etc. was motivated by the question "Does it slam the clam?" That is, does it help to beat Shell?[301]

An example of "naming a problem" but resorting to the emotion of pride is what a small American NGO called *Institute for Health Improvement* did. This NGO launched a media campaign called "100,000 Lives Campaign", intended to reduce deaths caused by mistakes in hospitals through simple procedures such as reminding nurses and doctors to *wash their hands and disinfect surgical items*, check food, and maintain general hygiene. Many deaths occur due to hospital-acquired infections that can be avoided through these simple procedures. To achieve its objective, the institute needed to generate a collective emotion in order to enthuse hospital executives to join the campaign and implement the measures recommended by this small NGO.

Before the campaign, the CEO of this NGO and his staff learned about the idea of "naming a problem" from writer and activist Gloria Steinem, who warned about a problem that had always occurred in the

United States but was not recognized or had nothing done to prevent it: those dates that ended in women being raped. "Date rape"[302] was the name she gave to this topic and this served to promote it in the media and get people to start talking about it. A name often helps people to understand a problem, given that the first connection with reality is its name, putting it into words. What is not named is as if it did not exist, it has no entity. Well, deaths in hospitals due to foreseeable errors are a serious problem, *but no one had named it, it had not been news in the media.*

Following the lesson they had learned from Gloria Steinem, this NGO organised the campaign and gave a shocking name to these hospital problems: "Preventable errors are killing too many people." The name "needless deaths" made many CEOs and hospital administrators join this campaign. If they did not adhere, they risked appearing to be "uncaring, immoral or incompetent" in the eyes of public opinion. To launch the campaign, they organised an event where a woman took the stage to tell how her 18-month-old daughter had died due to an error that could have been foreseen, in a highly prestigious hospital (Johns Hopkins Hospital). This campaign ended up saving 122,300 lives in just 2 years in 3,200 hospitals in the United States, a great achievement for a small NGO, and it was reached, in part, thanks to giving it a *name*.

Naming a problem is also what former Ford CEO Alan Mulally did in 2006. For decades there had been a very negative internal competition among executives at Ford. They sought to pit against each other. There was no incentive to share information or help one another. The result was that there was more competition within Ford than with other car manufacturers. Mulally noticed this negative atmosphere and named the problem by saying that he was going to "create just one team." When a journalist asked him if they were going to merge or unite with another company, Mulally responded "Yeah. We´re going to merge with ourselves."[303]

He began by taking measures such as putting Ford subsidiaries from different regions (Asia and Europe) under the same name and holding a meeting every Thursday during which he generated a positive, pleasant environment, so that executives openly discussed problems, including mistakes and failures. He made it clear that he would not allow aggressive attitudes and constantly reminded them that everyone had to collaborate and help each other. When the executives saw that cooperation was not a disadvantage for their careers at Ford, they slowly began to cooperate with each other. Even today Thursday meetings are overseen by an outsider who ensures that executives treat each other as friends rather than enemies, discussing problems openly and acting as members of "One Ford."

LA INNOVACION EN SILICON VALEY

> An innovation is the transformation of a new idea into sales.[304]
>
> A. G. Lafley
> (Procter & Gamble)

Chapter 7

Implementation

At the beginning of the book we said that innovation equals creativity plus implementation. We have seen what creativity is in the first chapters. Let us now focus on *implementation*. Some consultants have discovered from talking to many business owners and managers that they generally know what they need to do to make their companies as effective as possible and even make them innovative. However, they do not put it into practice. Consultants began to study this issue, sometimes called the gap between knowing and doing. In fact, there is a book on this gap, *The Know-Doing Gap: How Smart Companies Turn Knowledge into Action* (2000) by Jeffrey Pfeffer and Robert Sutton.

The consultants discovered many reasons for this dissociation between knowing and doing. At times it is due to poorly designed economic incentives, other times due to dysfunctional competition, or to a lack of resources or support from higher management. However, one of the most pervasive reasons found is what Pfeffer and Sutton call the "smart talk trap." This "trap" consists in talking about good ideas, talking intelligently about them, but then doing nothing to implement them. Some managers and executives who are very good speakers spread enthusiasm and have good ideas but do not implement them. Since they are charismatic or friendly, they get good bonuses and rewards at the end of the year, more than others who are quiet yet *prove their effectiveness through their actions*. In an interview, Sutton asked Brad Bird, director of Pixar films, who the people were who most hindered innovation and he replied: "People who talk quality but don't put it in their own work, yeah, it´s those types. You know, I don´t mind somebody who's green if they´re engaged, because I know they're on the hunt. But there are people who know the buzzwords of quality people, but don´t actually walk the walk."[305]

In my country (Argentina) we have a name for such characters: "verseros", smooth talkers. Why is this? The fact is that some companies reward people simply for what they say; they reward *image* but not effectiveness. We live in an age of images. Today's man is a "homo videns", one who is guided by what he sees, by the images on television. Politicians know this and that is why they kiss babies in front of the cameras, and millions of naive people vote for them thanks to these media gestures. In this day and age, many people find it difficult to distinguish between *talkers* and *doers* and this is also happening in teams and companies.

Measures to counteract the "smart talk trap"

To avoid this "trap", some measures can be taken says Sutton at a Stanford´s class. The first is to assign people who really understand the work that needs to be done. When people understand the job they are much less likely to have the defect of talking while doing nothing. An example of this is Anne Mulcahy of Xerox. There was a time when this large company was going through serious financial problems in addition to facing accusations of "improper financial management."

Instead of just talking smart, Mulcahy met with about 100 people at Xerox to hear what was wrong and she asked for help with the drastic reconversion they would have to make. She also spent time listening to hundreds of customers and lower-ranking employees. She asked her staff members to teach her financing as it was necessary for her to do a better job due to Xerox's debts. She remembers, "Folks in the controller´s department would spend hours with me just making sure I was prepared to answer all the ugly tough questions from bankers."[306] Mulcahy became CEO in 2001 – after holding several different positions at this company – and within a couple of years, Xerox began to be profitable again.

Another example is Bill George, Medtronic's CEO, credited with growing this medical products company from $1 billion in 1989 to $60 billion in 2002.[307] George was new to this industry. During the first nine months, he spent more than half his time visiting hospitals, looking at surgical equipment on which to install Medtronic products, as well as talking to patients, families and administrators. He also consulted surgeons and nurses. He then began to focus on the operational details for he felt he had to understand how Medtronic worked. Bill Gates, Steve Jobs and Elon Musk are also people with an understanding of the work being done and this is one of the hallmarks of great innovators. Therefore, understanding the work is crucial to avoid the "trap of speaking intelligently."

The second measure –says Sutton– is to dismantle negative environments as soon as possible, given that these are characterized by complaints, that is, by talking and not by implementing. As we have seen, some studies say that when people engage in a lot of complaining and other negative attitudes, they spread their bad mood and can reduce team performance by up to 40%. This makes it difficult to transform knowledge into action and creativity into implementation. One of the examples of dismantling a negative environment is what a woman named Annette Kyle did while managing 60 employees at a Celanse Corporation cargo terminal in Texas. Kyle led what she calls a "revolution" that consisted of several measures, changing the position and responsibilities of many people and modernizing measuring equipment on boats and trucks.

Kyle auctioned off her desk to the workers. She used to say "I shouldn't be sitting behind a desk; I should be out helping you."[308] When she arrived at the company, she noticed that there was a very negative atmosphere among the cargo terminal workers. So she had them sew a patch on their uniforms that said "No Whining," to remind them that if there was a problem, they had to report it to her but that the solution was not to complain about it. During her management, she managed to lower the cost of freight from 2.5 million dollars to less than ten thousand dollars. Before her arrival, it took workers an average of three hours to load a truck but after her "revolution" more than 90% of the trucks were loaded in one hour. Employee surveys and interviews also showed that they were more satisfied with their jobs and proud of what they had accomplished. In summary, reducing the amount of complaints and negativity are basic measures to facilitate or promote creativity in work teams.

The third measure is to use *simple instructions* since it is very difficult for people to work well when they are given orders or instructions in complicated or unclear language. Some teachers and academics, wanting to convince their students that they are intelligent, speak with complicated words that students do not understand. This is a way of giving people the impression that they are brilliant and sophisticated, a variant of the "smart talking trap." The point is that the most effective leaders use simple language and say the same thing over and over again, until it sticks in their teams' minds. A. G. Lafley, former CEO of Procter & Gamble, said the same thing over and over again in simple language. He constantly used the motto "Let's Keep it Simple" and phrases like "The customer is the boss" (Lafley's phrase was in "Keep it Sesame Street Simple" in reference to the Sesame Street cartoon series). Human beings, Lafley says, "tend not to stay focused. Therefore, my job is to get them to focus their creativity, productivity and efficiency on the objective."[309]

An example of why simple instructions help to turn knowledge into action can be seen in the movie *Sully*, about the pilot who made an emergency landing in the Hudson River (New York), a real event. Minutes before landing, the flight attendants kept repeating to the passengers: "Brace, brace, heads down, stay down."[310] The repetition of "hold on" was used because it has been studied that in stressful situations, people lose concentration and cannot follow the simplest instructions, unless these are repeated to them as if they were 5-year-olds.

Using simple instructions also decreases "cognitive load" as an experiment by Professor Baba Shiv (Stanford) demonstrated. This teacher brought together two groups of students. He gave the first group a 2-digit number to remember, while the second group was given a 7-digit number. He then told them to walk down a hallway where he presented two different food options to tempt them: a piece of chocolate cake or a healthy fruit salad. Students who remembered their 2 digits chose the fruit salad. On the other hand, those who made the effort to remember the 7 digits (higher "cognitive load") chose the "biggest prize", the chocolate cake[311]. The reason is that the additional digits took up valuable space in their brains, and due to the effort, made it *harder to resist the chocolate cake*. In short, all it took was five extra digits of information to tempt their brains with the cake.

Another example of simplicity was Steve Jobs. One of the best things he did as CEO when he returned to Apple in 1997 was to spend several weeks wandering around the company to find out what the product portfolio was. He would ask employees what the differences were between the 3400, 4400, 5400, and 6500 computer models. He discovered that Apple had so many different models that, Jobs recalls, "we couldn't even tell our friends which ones to buy."[312] This strategy confused Apple's customers, made it difficult to concentrate marketing and development efforts on so many products, and caused problems with suppliers. In one year, Jobs cancelled several products, leaving Apple with fewer models.

In a short time, Apple became profitable again and became the fantastic company that earned Jobs his reputation of a "creative genius." Even today, Apple has an incredibly small product portfolio: few computer models and the release of only one iPhone at a time, 9, 10, 12, 13, etc. Ultimately, the lesson that these innovators leave us is that when things are simple, people know how to focus their efforts better. When implementing, it is essential to simplify the instructions given to work teams.

Three final tips

The first piece of advice is that there is no way to innovate without failing. It is almost impossible to innovate without making mistakes, since innovation requires many attempts. As we have seen, it took James Dyson 5,127 prototypes before his bagless vacuum cleaner was ready for the market. The reason for the name of lubricant WD-40 is that the first 39 formulas failed while the 40th was successful, and Edison said, "I haven't failed... I just found 10,000 ways that don't work." A hallmark of good companies and innovation teams is their positive attitude towards people when they fail.

There are three different attitudes toward mistakes and failures, Sutton explains in a class at Stanford. The first is the worst and a kind of standard procedure in many companies: when people make mistakes, they resort to blaming and stigmatizing them: they are made to feel like children, they are humiliated, etc. They are not even taught a lesson, they are just made to feel bad. This attitude, which many arrogant managers and executives have, is not constructive and does not create an environment of psychological safety, which is essential to boost creativity.

The second is to *forgive* and *forget*. This attitude has some advantages: when a boss forgives, he provides some security and comfort. At the same time, however, if he forgets about the mistake, there is *no responsibility or learning whatsoever*. Forgive and forget is not a good leadership style either. Therefore, the most constructive attitude, says Sutton, is to *forgive and remember*: forgive so that there is psychological security and remember so as to learn from mistakes[313].

Of course there are some out there who never learn, who continue making the same mistakes over and over again even if they are forgiven and guided. When this happens, it is a sign that they should be doing something else. A good diagnostic question for a team or company to know if it has the right environment to innovate is "What happens when people make mistakes?" If the answer is 'forgive and remember', the environment is more conducive to innovation than in the first two options (blame and forget). "If you want to be inventive, you have to be willing to fail," says Jeff Bezos.[314] This does not mean that failure is good. On the contrary, it is bad, no one likes it but it is an inevitable part of life learning and doing innovative work.

The second piece of advice is that innovation requires *sales*. When you look at the history of great innovators, there are two things that stand out. One is that, in some way or other, they got great ideas from someone or somewhere and the second was that they managed to sell and market them very well. For example, Robert Fulton received all the credit for inventing the steamboat, yet by that time, in the 19th century, there were already many large —or at least functional— steamboats used in mining. However, the reason Fulton got all the credit and people bought his boats was that he, more than anyone else, was the best seller of this invention. A.G.Lafley, former CEO of Procter & Gamble states:

> Until people are willing to buy your product, pay for it, and then buy it again, there is no innovation. A gee whiz product that does not deliver value to the customer and provide financial benefit to the company is not an innovation. Innovation is not complete until it shows up in the financial results." [315]

Thomas Edison was not only a great inventor but also a wonderful salesman. Once, when a journalist went to his lab in New Jersey, Edison ran around to the back and put on dirty clothes, as if he had been inventing in his lab when, in fact, he had been doing something else. As the journalist was led inside,

> the Old Man disguised himself to resemble the heroic image of the "Great Inventor, Thomas Edison"… Suddenly gone were his natural boyishness of manner, his happy hooliganism. His features were frozen into immobility, he became statuesque in

the armchair, and his unblinking eyes assumed a faraway look.[316]

With this kind of gestures and publicity stunts, Edison propagated an image of the "lone genius" that journalism spread among the public. He was therefore a "wizard" of marketing and sales: he retired with 12 million dollars, a huge sum in his time. Steve Jobs was more the designer and marketer of Apple while his partner Wozniak was the technician and engineer. It is essential to consider what kind of people can form a company since you need individuals who can invent but can also *sell and obtain income*.

The last tip for being a good leader is to ask oneself if the people on a team are more or less energized after interacting with their boss. Some leaders spread enthusiasm and energize their team, while others simply discourage, mistreat or create obstacles. Some research by Professor Rob Cross (University of Virginia) supports this point. A few years ago, Cross and his colleagues were analysing who was the most effective versus the least effective leader using a very detailed questionnaire. Suddenly it occurred to them to ask, after talking to this person, "how does it typically affect your energy level?"[317] When they analysed the data from this study, it turned out that one of the most important factors in predicting whether a person would get a promotion or be surrounded by people who made efforts to innovate was how that simple question was answered.

Therefore, a question that a boss should ask himself if he wants to be a good innovation leader is, after people talk to me, do they have more or less energy? When people first hear this research, they think this means being more exciting, charismatic, or likable. But Cross's research shows that this is not the case, that energetic people are often a little low-key or perhaps boring. However, they do a lot of things we mentioned in previous chapters, such as watch their people's backs, creating situations in which people feel rewarded for their efforts, and knowing when to push hard enough but not too hard.

In particular, the study found that energetic bosses see more possibilities for innovation, while non-energetic bosses only see obstacles and problems. Energetic people make their team feel like they can contribute significantly to making things better, while non-energetic people believe that only they have the answer. Energetic people listen carefully when their people talk to them and this is seen in their body language, gestures, eyes, etc. On the other hand, the non-energetic ones only want to silence others and impose their point of view. Finally, the energetic ones are upright and clear, they have no hidden or selfish intentions – they tell the truth – while the others do just the opposite. The energy that a leader infects his team with is one of the most important traits that a boss or manager who intends to innovate must possess.

DIEGO F. WARTJES

LA INNOVACION EN SILICON VALEY

> When we see weird problems, it's likely that someone at IDEO has the capability to solve them.[318]
>
> **Steve Jobs**

Chapter 8

What is IDEO?

In previous chapters we referred to IDEO, a famous innovation consultancy in Silicon Valley. In 1980 Jobs asked IDEO to develop a *mouse* for a new computer, the Lisa. The IDEO team abandoned the expensive mechanism of the previous mouse and replaced it with a more practical component that is still used in practically all mouses today. Jobs remembers,

> I remember arguing with these folks, people screaming at me that it would take us five years to engineer a mouse and it would cost $300 to build. And I finally got fed up. I just went outside and found *David Kelley Design* [later renamed IDEO] and asked them to design me a mouse. And in 90 days we had a mouse we could build for 15 bucks that was phenomenally reliable.[319]

David Kelley and Steve Jobs worked together for over 30 years. Kelley remembers, Jobs "was such a good client. We did our best work for him. We became friends and he'd call me at 3 o'clock in the morning."[320] IDEO helped design dozens of products for Apple, including the Apple III and Lisa computers. In 2007, Kelley was diagnosed with throat cancer with a 40 percent chance of survival. Jobs, who was already suffering from his own deadly cancer, gave him some advice, "Look, you know, don't consider any alternative – go straight to Western medicine. Don't try any herbs or anything."[321] Jobs had tried to cure himself with alternative methods: natural juices, acupuncture and dietary supplements. One of the most important achievements of IDEO is that by means of their database (collected over 26 years on clients in different industries), they have discovered the 6 attributes of innovative companies. This discovery has made a fundamental contribution to understanding how innovation is generated. Before commenting on these 6 attributes, I will briefly describe the origin of IDEO and the way they work.

The origin of this consulting firm dates back to 1978 when engineer David Kelley, who had worked for aircraft manufacturer Boeing, set up his design firm, David Kelley Design (DKD). In 1991 David Kelley joined up with Bill Moggridge and Mike Nuttall. They merged their offices and called it IDEO, a word that in English means "ideas" and other derivatives such as "ideogram" and "ideology." They were later joined by David's brother, Tom Kelley.

IDEO's headquarters take up six buildings in downtown Palo Alto (Silicon Valley, California). They have branches in San Francisco, New York, Chicago, Boston, London, Munich, Shanghai and Tokyo (with approximately 600 employees by 2022). They have won more design awards than any other firm. In 2014 alone they won 8 awards from the *Industrial Designers Society of America*. Their clients range from multinationals to companies looking for the technical skills they lack.

Andrew Hargadon (UC Davies) says that IDEO have designed more than 4,000 products for 1,000 companies in more than 50 different industries. Among these products are laptop computers, toy guitars, medical equipment the size of small cars, children's toothbrushes, the mechanical whale for the movie Free Willy, water bottles for bicycles, interior design for the Amtrak high-speed train Acela, Leap chair for Steelcase, insulin pens for Eli Lilly, Palm V, Polaroid i-Zone instant camera, Nike sunglasses, Smith ski goggles, Logitech joysticks, Crest's Neat Squeeze toothpaste tube, e-books, surgical devices, etc.[322]

Since they are a consultancy specialized in creativity, their offices consist in open loft-like spaces with numerous products, prototypes, sketches, foam models and toys scattered everywhere. Upon entering their offices you get the impression of a mix of high technology and a nursery school (or kindergarten). IDEO are almost as well known for their creative process as for their innovative products. Although Alex F. Osborn (co-founder of the BBDO advertising agency) introduced brainstorming in 1953 with his book *Applied Imagination*, it was IDEO that made it famous, doing away with traditional management hierarchies and making the engineering process fun. The IDEO consulting firm are also expert in the creative process of *Design Thinking*. David Kelley is a professor and founder of the *Hasso Plattner Institute of Design* at Stanford University, known as the *d. school* to differentiate it from the business or *b. school*.

For each new project, IDEO use the experiences their engineers and designers have gained while working for clients in different industries. At IDEO the traditional bureaucratic hierarchy is practically non-existent. There may be a handful of "managers" who work together assigning people to projects. But even these managers spend time on engineering tasks to "keep their hands dirty." That does not mean there are no bosses or managers at IDEO. Even without a formal hierarchy, everyone knows who is the best designer, the best project leader, who to turn to for help, and who the boss is. It just means that there are no rigidly established hierarchies. For each project there is a project manager, a boss (the client) and on each team everyone has a clear role. In the following project, however, the previous manager might change and end up working for someone he managed the last time.

Depending on the nature of the problem, the client or the industry, different engineers or designers become experts. For a hair-cutting project, an engineer's experience with harvesting machines can be useful and so is then incorporated into the team. But for the next project, say, redesigning a tractor cab, this manager may take a more central role in the team. At IDEO it is rare for people to continue working in a particular industry for more than one or two projects. Teams often break up completely after a project. This movement gives people a wide range of experiences. Additional members are often brought in for brief brainstorming or temporary efforts.

Teams are typically small, averaging two to seven people, and their size over time depends on the demands of the project. This allows them to draw on the experiences and knowledge of different people. Sean Corcorran, manager of IDEO, has applied this changeable structure to an initiative called "the 15-minute move," creating offices whose furniture could be removed and rearranged in just 15 minutes, to adapt to the structure of each new team. The solution was to embed more plugs and power sockets in the floor so that the staff could reconfigure the space at will, with all the furniture on casters for them to slide, without having to put everything away or taking anything apart.

Hargadon says that IDEO designers have amassed a collection of more than 400 materials and products they keep in the *Tech Box*, a set of drawers and cabinets in each of IDEO's offices that house many of the mechanical and electrical gadgets they have worked with in the past: their projects, small batteries, switches, glow-in-the-dark fabric, flexible circuit boards, electric motors, speakers, holographic candy, flexible and elastic hinges, metal plating, vacuum-sealed copper tubes, plywood tubes, and so on. Every time someone sees or uses something that seems useful, they leave it in the *Tech Box*, register it, and put it up on a website. When a problem arises in a new project, designers can take what they need from the *Tech Box* for inspiration or as a solution.[323]

In addition to consulting in the most varied industries, IDEO has also ventured into education, creating innovative low-price schools in Peru. Peruvian businessman Carlos Rodríguez-Pastor, CEO of Intercorp (a group with more than 30 companies, banks, shopping centers, pharmacies, supermarkets, cinemas, etc., which represents 2.5% of Peru's gross domestic product), hired IDEO to build a complete network of private schools (*Innova*) driven by a new learning model. "The future of our country," says Rodríguez-Pastor, "is based on our ability to successfully educate the next generation. IDEO helped *Innova* design a school model that brings quality international education to Peru." *Innova* is a network of 54 private schools at an affordable cost for Peruvian families (USD 100 per month) with more than 2,000 teachers and over 43,000 students. In 2013, this network had already improved students' skills in mathematics and reading above Peru's national average.[324]

The 6 attributes of the most innovative companies in the world

For many years IDEO analysed more than 250 organisations and 500 work teams in 14 different countries and discovered that the most innovative companies in the world have 6 attributes in common: 1) they empower their members; 2) they carry out experiments to learn what works and what does not; 3) their work culture is based on creative collaboration; 4) they apply beauty and elegance to their products (e.g. Apple); 5) they look to other industries for ideas and 6) they have a clear purpose that inspires staff. Improving these attributes in more than 250 organisations resulted in performance 211 to 303 percent higher than the average of S&P 500 companies.[325]

After identifying these 6 attributes, IDEO created an assessment tool (*Creative Difference*), a survey that helps members of a company understand to what extent they are creative, flexible or competitive. The survey invites all members to give feedback on their work experiences. IDEO analyse this information and provide a complete analysis of the team or company's performance together with feedback on measures to implement to drive innovation. For example, the survey may show that a team has a very clear *purpose* but lacks collaboration. A team may score high on *empowerment* while very poorly or even not at all on *experimentation*.

More than 100 companies have used *Creative Difference* to assess their teams' skills. In Latin America, for instance, the Peruvian group Intercorp was faced with the challenge of acquiring innovation skills.

Intercorp Chief Innovation Officer Hernán Carranza says that *Creative Difference*: "… is our master tool to maximise the creativity of our 58,000 employees and track how our 29 companies evolve year after year. It is measurable, scalable and extremely actionable."[326] Thanks to this tool, Intercorp managed to launch 5 new digital services in 2018.

What do these 6 attributes consist of? We have commented on some of these attributes in preceding chapters but it is now worth complementing them with IDEO's vision. *Empowerment*, the first attribute in order of impact, takes place when managers give teams freedom to solve problems, supporting them when they take risks, and allowing people to feel comfortable challenging the *status quo*. According to IDEO, organisations where members feel *empowered* are 69% more likely to launch products and services to market successfully. In other words, *empowering* means giving power to people. How is this done? Giving them *freedom* to put forward ideas and take the initiative, without anyone punishing, mocking or ridiculing them.

The second attribute in order of impact is *experimentation*. IDEO has found that teams that test 5 or more alternative solutions are 50% more likely to launch successful products or services. Innovative companies carry out experiments to test new ideas and products, they have little bureaucracy and a constructive attitude towards failures, knowing that some will be necessary to discover new opportunities. They build prototypes quickly and cheaply to explore new ideas and concepts and share the ideas with each other. Experimentation is essential for organisations to obtain feedback from their customers and end users.

In their book *Creative Confidence* (2013), Tom Kelley and David Kelley comment that experimentation is the origin of many innovations throughout history. Thomas Edison said that "the real measure of success is the number of experiments that can be crowded into twenty-four hours." The Kelleys were born in Ohio where the Wright brothers achieved the first flight of an airplane in 1903, yet focusing on this historic flight makes us forget the "hundreds of experiments and failed flight trials in the years that led up to that first successful flight."³²⁷ Charles Goodyear did many experiments until he discovered the best way to treat rubber, the material used today to make Goodyear tyres. The Kelleys point out that the best way to accomplish something is to:

> build a prototype... If you show up at a meeting with an interesting prototype while others bring only a laptop or a yellow pad, don't be surprised if the whole meeting is centered around *your* ideas. The reason for prototyping is experimentation, the act of creating of forces you to ask questions and make choices. It also gives you something you can show and talk about with other people. We often build physical prototypes.³²⁸

Being open to experimentation is what often leads to innovation, as in the case of Air New Zealand. Due to its isolation in the southern hemisphere, very far from air routes to London or Los Angeles, they were forced to give their flights some added value, such as more comfortable seats. So Air New Zealand teamed up with a team from IDEO to generate some ideas. They brainstormed and produced a dozen unconventional prototypes, from harnesses to keep passengers upright, to a group of seats facing each other arranged around a table and even hammocks hanging from the ceiling. Since everyone actively participated, no one was afraid of feeling judged or criticised. Ed Sims, general manager of Air New Zealand, recalls, "It was liberating getting on the floor with cardboard, polystyrene, and paper, cutting seat concepts."³²⁹

Being open to the craziest ideas and questioning beliefs, they developed Skycouch, economy class seats that allow one to lie down. The seats include a padded footrest that can be folded up, allowing a row of three seats to turn into a futon-like platform where passengers can recline or sleep. Area industry observers today call it the "cuddle class." This new design, the result of experimentation, earned Air New Zealand many awards, such as the *Condé Nast Traveler's Innovation & Design* award.

Experiments in the business world used to be carried out internally, behind closed doors. However, today innovative companies launch new products "to learn." Instead of waiting for the product to be fully developed, they launch it on the market to test it and obtain customer feedback to improve it. Many start-ups use this strategy. They do some designing, some implementation and release it still unfinished. They then introduce corrections and release it again. When they learn something that doesn't work, they modify it as quickly as possible. By launching a series of small experiments to learn, they avoid the risk of spending years perfecting a product that in the end no one will want. IDEO design director Tom Hulme describes it thus, "Release your idea into the wild before it's ready" because market testing, even when it is not finished, provides valuable information.[330]

This strategy is also used by innovative companies such as Google and Amazon. Google's philosophy is to launch products "early and constantly." Marissa Mayer (Google's former Vice President of Search Products) says,

> The *Googly* thing is to launch it early on Google Labs and then iterate, learning what the market wants–and making it great. The beauty of *experimenting* in this way is that you never get too far from what the market wants. The market pulls you back.[331]

Jeff Bezos knows how important each Amazon interaction with the customer is, i.e. the time it takes to enter your page, the ease of use, the speed to deliver packages, the quick response to customer emails, etc. Amazon's WebLab team are constantly experimenting with the user interface of their website. Statistical data shows them which interfaces work best.[332]

The third attribute in order of impact is *collaboration*. In a creative collaboration environment, all members of an organisation work together toward the same goal instead of competing with other divisions with a *silo* mentality (withholding information or refusing to help other divisions). We have seen that the difference between

Apple's success in launching their *iPod* and Sony's failure with their *Connect* was that at Apple there was a great spirit of collaboration while at Sony the *silo* mentality predominated.

IDEO have found that organisations where teams collaborate effectively are 38% more likely to launch successful products and services. Organisations where a spirit of collaboration reigns tend to create multidisciplinary teams to address problems. People feel comfortable looking to others for help while information is accessible to everyone in the company.

IDEO's best ideas have resulted from collaboration between several people. Creativity at IDEO is teamwork, like a sport. Yet collaborating with others requires humility. "You have to start by admitting –the Kelley brothers say– that you don't have all the answers." What IDEO has discovered after many years working for the world's most demanding clients is that the whole is better than the sum of the parts. To make teams work well, people have to adhere to the idea that working together is the best strategy and that no single person is entirely responsible for the ultimate success. Instead of individuals talking about "their ideas," the best teams feel more comfortable with the *group authorship* of ideas.

When a client recently "asked the members of one of our project teams to write their names on each of their Post-its in an ideation session, as a way of assigning credit, we really struggled. We were so accustomed to fluidly building directly on each other´s ideas in that setting, it felt really countercultural to say *This one is mine*"[333]. Collaboration works especially well when team members have different professions, knowledge and skills. That is why IDEO mixes engineers, anthropologists and business people with surgeons, nutritional scientists and economists who study human behaviour. By working in multidisciplinary teams, they can reach places they could never reach working individually.

IDEO consider that *creative duos* or *pairs* are very important for a team, because they transmit the trust they have in each other to the rest of the team.[334] Furthermore, every good team begins with a relationship between two people –the smallest number in a relationship. In management, individuals (CEOs as individual "heroes") or teams are often studied, while *duos are overlooked*, yet the history of innovation is full of notable duos: Jobs-Wozniak (Apple), Gates-Allen (Microsoft), Page-Brin (Google), Noyce-Moore (Intel), David Kelley-Tom Kelley (IDEO), Hewlett-Packard (HP), Wilbur and Oliver Wright (aviation pioneers), Edison-Batchelor, etc. The same is true in music: Lennon-McCartney (Beatles), Jagger-Richards (Rolling Stones), Elton John-Bernie Taupin, Richard and Karen Carpenter (The Carpenters), and so on.

The fourth attribute in order of impact is *implementation*. According to IDEO, organisations that are able to combine strategy, design, product and implementation harmoniously are 25% more likely to launch successful products and services. These organisations find elegant solutions to technical obstacles and the various company divisions communicate well from the initial vision up to the final implementation. Teams have the skills to overcome technical challenges during implementation and have enough time to solve these problems creatively. The search for solutions is not suspended or cancelled due to technical challenges that appear as insurmountable. Detailed work is considered a value and the organisation provides the conditions for people to be detailed in their work. Apple is the example of this, which can be seen in the elegance, design and finish of their products.

The fifth attribute of the most innovative organisations is that they *look to other industries for ideas*, what IDEO calls "Analogous Inspiration." Organisations that do this are 24% more likely to launch successful products and services. This attribute is about the degree to which employees obtain ideas and inspiration from beyond the company walls. This allows them to discover ideas and solutions to develop new products or services in their industry. Organisations that stand out for this have a clear idea of who their customers are, what is happening in the market and what trends (technical or sociological) they can take advantage of to achieve their objectives.

They research technologies relevant to their business, market trends and other industries and use them to find new opportunities. IDEO IS an example of this because to surprise their clients, they look at solutions and innovations in other industries. As we have seen, bicycle maker *Specialized* asked IDEO to design an original water bottle, and the IDEO team came up with the idea of using a spill-proof spout they had developed five years earlier for a shampoo bottle that could be hung upside down in the shower. They had learned about this mechanism when they worked for a company in the medical industry where they saw valves for artificial hearts. In short, looking at the shampoo and medical valve industries they extracted ideas to make water bottles for cyclists, a classic example of "inspiration by analogy."

The sixth attribute in order of impact is *purpose*. The most innovative organisations have a clear vision of why and for what they exist, apart from making money. This is what IDEO call their *purpose*. IDEO found that these organisations infuse their members with passion and are 20% more likely to launch successful new products and services. They are also 40% better at retaining talented people.[335] In organisations with a *clear purpose* the leadership and other staff are aligned in terms of the change they want to achieve. What is *purpose*? Purpose can be viewed from a personal perspective rather than a professional one. According to some studies, people who have a clear purpose in their lives live 15% longer than those who do not perceive any. Sometimes this purpose coincides with professional life.[336]

Purpose can also be generated in work teams. Some studies have proved it. For example, Professor Adam Grant (University of Pennsylvania, Wharton School) and colleagues arranged for a team of employees from a call centre –that was raising money for students in need to pay for their studies– to meet those students in a meeting just 5 minutes long. This brief encounter had a profound effect. Those who interacted with students went on to spend more than double the time on the phone and raised almost three times the weekly average ($503, initially $185).[337] Meeting these students motivated them to work longer and raise more money. Grant carried out studies in other industries and found the same result. His conclusion was that when people see the impact their work has and those they help, they are not only happier but more productive. Helping someone fulfil their dream motivated them to work harder. According to another study, 84% of millennials estimate that "making a difference" is more important than professional recognition, something that was also found in studies with adults.

Many companies state their *purpose* clearly and this helps them inspire their staff. For example, Tesla's purpose or mission, in terms of their electric cars, is to make the public live in a world of "sustainable energy" and has therefore made their invention patents available to the public. Elon Musk, the founder of Tesla, maintains,

> Technological leadership is not defined by patents but by a company's ability to attract the most talented engineers. We believe that opening our patents to the public will strengthen —rather than diminish— Tesla's position in this regard.[338]

Not only do Tesla state their purpose clearly, they also back it up with facts. They make their technology and patents known because they believe they contribute to a better world and this inspires many Tesla employees and customers, beyond money and cars per se. In 2014, Elon Musk said: "If we can do things that don't hurt us and help the U.S. industry, we should do that."[339]

Consultant Simon Sinek points out that many companies can explain what they do, some can explain how they do it but very few can explain "why they do what they do" (their purpose). The why is decisive for understanding human behaviour and reasoning – a distinctive feature of human beings. It seeks to understand why things happen or why someone said what they said or behaved in a certain way. Apple is a company that explains well why they do what they do. They have the formula to infuse their employees and clients with purpose and passion. Sinek points out,

If Apple were like everyone else, a marketing message from them might sound like this: "We make great computers. They're beautifully designed, simple to use and user friendly. Want to buy one?" And that's how most of us communicate. That's how most marketing is done, that's how most sales is done and that's how most of us communicate interpersonally. We say what we do, we say how we're different or how we're better and we expect some sort of a behavior, a purchase, a vote, something like that. (...) Here's how Apple actually communicates. "Everything we do, we believe in challenging the *status quo*. We believe in thinking differently. The way we challenge the *status quo* is by making our products beautifully designed, simple to use and user friendly. We just happen to make great computers. Want to buy one?" Totally different right? You're ready to buy a computer from me. All I did was reverse the order of the information. What it proves to us is that people don't buy what you do; *people buy why you do it.* (...) The goal is not to do business with everybody who needs what you have. The goal is to do business with people *who believe what you believe* (...) I always say that, you know, if you hire people just because they can do a job, they'll work for your money, but if you hire people *who believe what you believe,* they'll work for you with *blood and sweat and tears.* [340]

In conclusion, today all organisations face a volatile, uncertain, complex and ambiguous context (acronym *VUCA*) with difficult-to-solve problems that require multidisciplinary solutions (the term VUCA originated in the US army and in the works of Warren Bennis and Burt Namus, professors of business leadership).[341] Some studies maintain that in the next 10 to 20 years, around half the companies in the S&P 500 will be replaced by new companies with disruptive technologies, something that has already happened.[342] Indeed, during the decades from 1970 to 1990, several companies with disruptive technologies and business models displaced consolidated companies. As we have seen, Apple and their personal computer began to compete with IBM (*mainframes* and big computers for the government and large companies) while digital photography dethroned Kodak's monopoly of photograph rolls.

In the 2010s, Amazon already had approximately half of the printed book market. They had 84% of the market in *e-books*, while Barnes & Nobles (the largest publisher in the United States) had a mere 2%. Since 2010, Barnes & Nobles had to close some 90 stores.[343] Tesla, Elon Musk's company, dominate the electric car market in the United States, surpassing traditionally established companies such as Nissan, Chevrolet, Ford and Volkswagen. According to some reports, Tesla have a market share of 69.95% with Nissan in second place with 8.51%.[344] These cases show that any organisation —no matter how technologically advanced or consolidated it may be today— can be taken by surprise and surpassed by an entrepreneur, the next Jeff Bezos or Elon Musk. No one can "rest on their laurels." Therefore, it is advisable for organisations intending to remain in the market in the long term, to implement these 6 attributes discovered by IDEO (or improve on them if they already have them) in order to create an environment conducive to continuous innovation.

Conclusion

Innovation leadership in the 21st century

If you were appointed head of a group of people to do something innovative, for example, to manufacture a new product, different from all those offered on the market, what advice would you receive from Silicon Valley innovators? Let's assume you could choose your work team. The first piece of advice would be to choose people who not only have the knowledge but also empathy and a great willingness to work as part of a team (in Silicon Valley they call them T-Shape people). Remember that developing an innovative product requires the collaboration of many people, not just the contribution of "lone geniuses." Steve Jobs and Bill Gates said that everything done at Apple and Microsoft was done by talented people, with whom they partnered. On the other hand, the objective of creativity (the "big idea") is *to transform it into a product to sell to the public*. Therefore, it is important to have on your team people with the ability to sell, who know about marketing and advertising. Don't forget that Edison or Jobs were great creatives but marketing "wizards" as well.

Second, Silicon Valley innovators would also advise you to *empower* employees to propose solutions and make decisions, since companies where people feel *empowered* are 69% more likely to bring successful products to market (according to IDEO). "Our super power at Microsoft is our culture of empowering others," said Kevin Scott (Chief Technoloy Officer) at a conference in 2019 in Silicon Valley.[345] Never impose your hierarchy or your ego. Let the best ideas prevail, no matter who they come from. Listen humbly. Don't assume you know more than your subordinates.

Humility is one of the most valuable virtues while pride is one of the worst human defects. Stand up for what you believe in with conviction, but *listen to your team as if you were wrong*. When you hold meetings to discuss ideas, don't let them criticize the person who is proposing something, no matter how "silly" they may sound. Use your leadership to make them feel comfortable, for there are people who tolerate criticism without consequences, but others (more sensitive or introverted) may remain inhibited forever if they are harshly criticized.

Third, use your emotional intelligence – not just your "cold" rationality – to create a *psychologically safe* work environment: the most important aspect in Google Teams. Let everyone feel they can speak without fear of being ridiculed or punished. This will encourage them to propose ideas or approach you in confidence, to anticipate problems that you may be unaware of and could even prevent a crisis, or your dismissal as boss. The people on your team are the best allies in your job. But you are responsible for making them feel as "allies" rather than enemies or insignificant beings who know nothing and are there to obey you.

Fourth, quickly stop negativity in your work group, since innovating is difficult and negativity makes it even harder. Sometimes it just takes "one bad apple in the box" (one who always complains) to discourage the rest of the group or for others to imitate their bad attitudes. These have much more impact than the good ones. Each negative argument with your wife or partner requires 5 good conversations to repair it and sometimes an insult may never be forgotten. As we have seen, one boss made the decision to sew a "No Whining" patch on employees' uniforms to make it clear that, if there was a problem, they had to report it or propose a solution but not spread negativity.

Fifth, "open up the game" so that all staff are aware of the issues and challenges facing you, the company, or the department. It is vital to leverage the knowledge of all employees, not just other bosses, managers or shareholders (owners). No president or CEO – not even

Jobs or Gates – knows everything, no matter how brilliant they may be. A group of people is a wealth of collective intelligence or "dispersed knowledge," as the great economist F. Hayek would say.

Therefore, innovative companies implement methods for employees and even customers to propose ideas. For example, car manufacturer BMW has an internal social network called *Red Square* for employees to propose solutions and discuss them openly. Anonymous participation is allowed because otherwise no employee would dare to openly contradict their boss. It is currently used by more than 3,000 users who have discussed more than 2,000 ideas. Skytech's Thomas Geyer, who developed this social network for BMW, explains that,

> In order to enable the use of collective intelligence, environments are needed where people can communicate and interact across organizational boundaries free of fear and regulations.[346]

In this way, it is possible to avoid or lower the barriers of lack of communication and coordination which are naturally generated among the different departments in a company (*silos*). BMW bosses and leaders also get ideas from suppliers and customers through another tool: the *Customer Innovation Lab* (a virtual toolkit on the Internet). Many suppliers and BMW car fans have submitted hundreds of ideas on the most varied topics in this virtual innovation laboratory. For example, the idea of automatically transmitting relevant data to the insurance company in the event of an accident or informing the driver of the speed limits when entering a new country.

The Kelley brothers (IDEO) maintain that the,

> most innovative companies in the twenty-first century have transitioned from command-control organisations to a participatory approach that involves collaboration and teamwork. They draw on the whole brain of the company, gathering the best ideas and insights wherever they find them.

They are open to listening to people from the front line of their operation (...) Is there an employee just waiting for the right opportunity or partner to unlock billion of dollars value for your organization? Why not set up a process or system of participation that allows those building innovators to express their ideas? Why not give the members on your team or organisation more creative license, more of a chance to reach their full potential? (...) You might discover that someone you hadn't noticed before who is poised for greatness. Toyota stays among the top automotive companies in the world by empowering every single employee to propose innovations as intrinsic part of his or her job.[347]

Another measure that you can implement, if you have the space in your office, is to set up a "creativity room" with comfortable armchairs, candy and soft drinks vending machines, or ping pong, pool or foosball tables, where your workers will be encouraged to talk more freely and spontaneously, with you and among themselves. We have seen that Corning, the company that made the glass for Edison light bulbs, has a "creativity room." So go ahead and copy the good measures other companies take. We all learn by watching others. To learn how to play tennis, we watch videos of Roger Federer and for soccer, those of Messi.

Sixth, carry out experiments, even if they are small or "silly", as they can provide solutions or different approaches to address problems. Of all the *creative skills* Silicon Valley innovators have, *experimentation* is the most important. Strive to reduce your cost so you can increase the quantity (e.g. doing a survey of your clients or inviting them to a field day to listen to their suggestions are "experiments", a starting point). Without experimentation, there is no innovation. We have seen that the name of the WD-40 lubricant comes from the first 39 formulas that failed, which led to the successful 40th.

Michael Dell discovered his "business model" by taking computers apart to see how they worked, and according to IDEO, *experimentation* is the second most important attribute of innovative companies, after *empowerment*. Today, innovative companies do not wait to have a completely finished product before launching it on the market. On the contrary, they build prototypes quickly to obtain feedback from clients and end users. "We often can get a sense of just how good a new concept is if we only prototype for a single day or week," says Marissa Mayer (Google).[348]

This leadership style (Packard and Noyce's legacy) is the one with the best chance of making the people in charge feel happy and, as we have seen, happiness facilitates creativity.[349] When they are relaxed, studies show that they are more creative (on the other hand, people who are unhappy or under negative pressure are less creative). This leadership (short distance to power, with autonomy, empowerment, psychological safety and freedom) is what has generated the largest number of invention patents, managing to turn good ideas into products that the public desires and buys (sales go up!).[350] If you are the leader of a group of people who want to innovate, start here and never stop persevering in the face of successive failures.

Reference List

Books

Asakura, R. (2000): *Revolutionaries at Sony*, New York: McGraw-Hill.

Bachrach, E. (2012): *AgilMente*, Buenos Aires: Sudamericana.

Bachrach, E. (2012): *EnCambio*, Buenos Aires: Sudamericana.

Barnett, H. (1953): *Innovation: The Basis of Cultural Change*, Nueva York.

Berkun, S. (2010): *The Myths of Innovation*, Sebastopol (Canadá): O'Reilly Media.

Bennis, W., and Namus, B. (1985): *Leaders: The Strategies for Taking Charge*, Harpercollins. US Army Heritage and Education Center.

Berlin, L. (2006): *The Man behind the Microchip: Robert Noyce and the Invention of Silicon Valley*, New York: Oxford University Press.

Byers, T., Dorf, R., and Nelson, A. (2015): *Technology Ventures: From Idea To Enterprise*, New York: McGraw Hill.

Christensen, C. (1997): *The Innovator's Dilemma: When New Technologies Cause Great Firms to Fail*, Boston: Harvard Business School Press.

Damasio, A. (2003): *El error de Descartes*, Buenos Aires: Paidós.

Drucker, P. (1987): *La innovación y el empresario innovador*, Buenos Aires: Sudamericana.

Duckworth, A. (2016): *Grit, The Power of Passion and Perseverance*, New York: Simon & Schuster.

Dyer, J., Gregersen, H., and Christensen, C. (2011): *The Innovator's DNA: Mastering the Five Skills of Disruptive Innovators*, Boston: Harvard Business Review Press.

Gallo, C. (2011): *The Innovation Secrets of Steve Jobs*, New York: McGraw-Hill.

Gordon, J. S. (2001): *The Business of America: Tales from the Marketplace-American Enterprise from the Settling of New England to the Breakup of AT&T*, New York: Walker & Company.

Gupta, P. (2007): *Business Innovation in the 21 Century*, South Carolina: BookSurge, LLC, An Amazon Company.

Hackman, R. (2002): *Leading Teams*, Boston: Harvard Business School Press.

Hansen, M. (2009): *Collaboration*, Harvard Business School Publishing: Boston.

Hargadon, A. (2003): *How Breakthroughs Happen: The Surprising Truth About How Companies Innovate*, Boston: Harvard Business School Press.

Hofstede, G., Hofstede, G. J., and Minkow, M. (2010): *Culture and Organizations (Software of the Mind), Intercultural Cooperation and Its Importance for Survival*, United States, 3rd. ed.

Hounshell, D. (1984): *From the American System to Mass Production, 1800-1932: The Development of Manufacturing Technology in the United States*, Baltimore: Johns Hopkins University Press.

Isaacson, W. (2014): *Los innovadores*, Buenos Aires: Debate.

Johansson, F. (2004): *The Medici Effect*, Boston: Harvard Business School Publishing.

Kelley, T. (2005): *The Art of Innovation*, New York: Doubleday.

Kelley, T., and Kelley, D. (2013): *Creative Confidence*, New York: Random House.

Kirton, M. (1989). *Adaptors and Innovators: Styles of Creativity and Problem Solving* (Revised Edition). London: Routledge.

Khun, T. (1970): *The Structure of Scientific Revolutions* (Second Edition, Enlarged), Thomas S. International Encyclopedia of Unified Science Volumes I and II-Foundations of the Unity of Science Volume II-Number 2, The University of Chicago Press, 1970.

Kotter, J. and Cohen, D. (2002): *The Heart of Change*, Boston: Harvard Business Review Press.

Lafley, A. G., and Charan, R. (2008): *Game Changer*, New York: Random House.

Levy, S. (2007): *The Perfect Thing: How the iPod Shuffles Commerce, Culture, and Coolness*, New York: Simon & Schuster.

Lopez Rosetti, D. (2017): *Emoción y sentimientos*, Buenos Aires: Planeta.

Mass, P. (1999): *The Terrible Hours: The Man Behind the Greatest Submarine Rescue in History*, New York: HarperCollins.

Mendonca, L., Kirkland, R., and Kuntz, M. (2009): *What Matters? Ten Questions That Will Shape Our Future*, McKinsey Management Institute.

Michalko, M. (2001): *Craking Creativity*, Berkeley: Ten Speed Press.

Mueller, W. (1962): *The Rate and Direction of Inventive Activity: Economic and Social Factors*, Princeton.

Oppenheimer, A. (2014): *¡Crear o Morir!*, Buenos Aires: Sudamericana.

Ortega y Gasset, J. (1983): *Obras completas* Tomo I (1902-1916), Glosas, De la crítica personal, Madrid: Revista de Occidente.

Packard, D. (1995): *The HP Way: How Bill Hewlett and I Built Our Company*, New York: HarperBusiness.

Pink, D. (2009): *Drive, The Surprising Truth About What Motivates Us*, New York: Riverhead Book.

Rabinow, P. (1996): *Making PCR: A Story of Biotechnology*, Chicago: University of Chicago Press.

Reid, R. (1997): *Architects of the Web: 1,000 Days that Built the Future of Business*, New York: Wiley.

Rogers, S. (2002): *The Entrepreneur's Guide to Finance and Business.* McGraw Hill.

Sala-i-Martin, X. (2016): *Economía en colores*, Barcelona: Penguin Random House.

Segaller, S. (1998): *Nerds 2.0.1.: A Brief History of the Internet*, New York: TV Books.

Shultz, H., and Yang, D. (1997): *Pour Your Heart Into It: How Starbucks Built a Company One Cup at a Time*, New York: Hyperion.

Sigafoos, R. (1983): *Absolutely, Positively Overnight!*, Memphis: St. Luke´s Press.

Simonton, D. K. (1999). *Origins of genius: Darwinian perspectives on creativity*. Oxford University Press.

Spitzer, Q., and Evans, R. (1997): *Heads, You Win! How the Best Companies Think*, New York: Simon and Schuster.

Sutton, R. (2002): *Weird Ideas That Work*, New York: Free Press.

Sutton, R., and Rao, H. (2014): *Scalling Up Excellence*, New York: Random House.

Tellis, G. (2013): *Unrelenting Innovation, How to Build a Culture for Market Dominance*, San Francisco: Wiley & Sons.

Townsend, R. (2007): *Up the Organization*, San Francisco: Jossey-Bass, 1970.

Wentz, R. C. (2012): *The Innovation Machine*, Alemania: Amazon.

Articles, studies (journals), papers, and interviews

A Century of Innovation, The 3M Story, International Standard Book, 2002. Available at: http://multimedia.3m.com.

About IDEO. Available at: https://www.ideo.com/about.

"Arthur Rock, MBA 1951", Harvard Business Review. Available at: https://entrepreneurship.hbs.edu/founders/Pages/profile.aspx?num=24.

"A Dozen Things I've Learned from Marissa Mayer about Business, Management, and Innovation", 25ip, December 14, 2014. Available at: https://25ip.com/2014.

Alaban, L. (2021): "San Jose Legends: John Sobrato's generosity is everywhere", *San José Spotlight*, June 27, 2021. Available at: https://sanjosespotlight.com/san-jose-legends-john-sobratos-generosity-is-everywhere/.

Amabile T., Hadley, C., and Kramer, S. (2002): "Creativity Under the Gun", Harvard Business Review, August 2002. Available at: https://hbr.org/2002/08/creativity-under-the-gun.

Amabile, T., and Kramer, S. (2011): *The Progress Principle: Using Small Wins to Ignite Joy, Engagement, and Creativity at Work*, Boston, Harvard Business School Publishing. Available at: https://www.hbs.edu/faculty/Pages/item.aspx?num=40692.

Andersen, E. (2013): "21 Quotes From Henry Ford On Business, Leadership And Life", *Forbes*, May 31, 2013. Available at: https://www.forbes.com/sites/erikaandersen/2013/05/31/21-quotes-from-henry-ford-on-business-leadership-and-life/.

"Annacone, el guía espiritual de Sampras y Federer", *La Nación*, Buenos Aires, August 1, 2019. Available at: https://www.lanacion.com.ar/deportes/annacone-guia-espiritual-sampras-federer-nid2273088/.

Answers.com, "Jeff Bezos", May 2003. Available at: http://www.answers.com/topic/jeff bezos.

Auletta, K. (2011): "Can Sheryl Sandberg Change Silicon Valley?" (A Woman´s Place), *The New Yorker*. July 4, 2011. Available at: https://www.newyorker.com/magazine/2011/07/11/a-womans-place-ken-auletta.

Baard, P., Deci, E., and Ryan, R. (2004): "Intrinsic Need Satisfaction: A Motivational Basis of Performance and Well-Being in Two Work Settings". *Journal of Applied Social Psychology*, 34, 2045-2068. http://dx.doi.org/10.1111/j.1559-1816.2004.tb02690.x.

Bartlett, C., and Ghoshal, S. (2002): "Building Competitive Advange through People". *MIT Sloan Management Review* (Winter).

Barr, J. (2015): "Doug Klunder '81 Excel creator works for civil liberties", *MIT Technology Review*, December 22, 2015. Available at: https://www.technologyreview.com/s/543961/doug-klunder-81/.

Bennis, W. y Namus, B. (1985): *Leaders: The Strategies for Taking Charge*, Harpercollins. US Army Heritage and Education Center. Q. Who first originated the term VUCA (Volatility, Uncertainty, Complexity and Ambiguity)?. Available at: https://usawc.libanswers.com/faq/84869.

"Best Practices in State and Regional Innovation Initiatives: Competing in the 21st Century", V. Annex A Stanford and Silicon Valley, National Academy of Sciences, 2013. Available at: https://www.ncbi.nlm.nih.gov/books/NBK158815/.

Bezos quote. "Quotefancy". Available at: https://quotefancy.com/quote/1093142/Jeff-Bezos-If-you-want-to-be-inventive-you-have-to-be-willing-to-fail.

Bluedorn A., Turban, D., and Love, M. (1999): "The Effects of Stand-Up and Sit-Down Meeting Formats on Meeting Outcomes", *Journal of Applied Psychology* 84 (1999): 277-285.

Boltgroup (2016): "You Manage Things; You Lead People", August 16, 2016. Available at: https://boltgroup.com/manage-things-lead-people/.

Brown, J. (IDEO): *The Power of Purpose* en IDEO University. Available at: https://www.ideou.com/pages/course-calendar.

Bryant, A. (2009): "Linda Hudson of BAE on Fitting In, and Rising to the Top", *The New York Times* (Corner Office), September, 19 2009. Available at: https://www.nytimes.com/2009/09/20/business/20corner.html.

Campbell, D. (1960): "Blind Variation and Selective Retention in Creative Thought as in Other Knowledge Processes", *Psychological Review* 67, no.6 (1960): 380-400.

Carpenter, M., Sanders, G., and Gregersen, H. (2001): "Building Human Capital: The Impact of International Assignment Experience on CEO Pay and Multinational Firm Performance", *Academy of Management Journal* 44, no. 3 (2001): 493-512.

Carringer, D.C. (1974): "Creative Thinking Abilities in Mexican Youth", *Journal of Cross-Cultural Psychology* 5 (1974): 492-504.

Catmull, E., and Wallace, A. (2014): "Creativity, Inc.: Overcoming the Unseen Forces That Stand in the Way of True Inspiration". Available at: https://highlights.sawyerh.com/volumes/a1351c21-deba-45a0-9ec2-6322200c1753.

Claire, M. (2014): "Shaping a School System from the Ground Up", *The New York Times,* July 5, 2014. Available at: https://ed.stanford.edu/in-the-media/shaping-school-system-ground-quotes-sandy-speicher-gse-alumna.

Clark Scott, D. (2011): "Robert Noyce: "Why Steve Jobs idolized Noyce", *The Christian Science Monitor,* December 12, 2011. Available at: https://www.csmonitor.com/Technology/2011/1212/Robert-Noyce-Why-Steve-Jobs-idolized-Noyce.

Colligan, M., Pennebaker, J., and Murphy, L. (1982): *Mass Psychogenic Illness: A Social Psychological Analysis,* Hillsdale, NJ, Erlbaum.

"Communication: Keep it Simple", Leading Blog: A Leadership Blog". Available at: https://www.leadershipnow.com/leadingblog/2008/10/communication_keep_it_simple.html.

"Como lograr estos 6 atributos que poseen las empresas mas innovadoras del mundo", *El Cronista,* June 19, 2019 (entrevista a Gonzalo Wartjes).

Cornell University, INSEAD, and WIPO (2015): "The Global Innovation Index 2015: Effective Innovation Policies for Development", Fontainebleau, Ithaca, and Geneva.

Cross R., Rebele, R., and Grant, A. (2016): "Collaborative Overload", Harvard Business Review, January-February 2016. Available at: https://hbr.org/2016/01/collaborative-overload.

Cross R., Baker, W., and Parker, A. (2003): "What creates energy in organizations?", *MIT Sloan Management Review*, June 2003.

Cummings, A., and Oldham, G. (1997): "Enhancing Creativity: Managing Work Contexts for the High Potential Employee", *California Management Review* 40 (1997): 22-38.

"David Packard´s 11 Simple Rules", HP Retiree. Available at: http://www.hp.com/retiree/history/founders/packard/11rules.html

del Bono, T. (2003): "La fuga de cerebros pone en riesgo el futuro", *La Nación*, Buenos Aires, November, 12 2003. Available at: https://www.lanacion.com.ar/opinion/la-fuga-de-cerebros-pone-en-riesgo-el-futuro-nid544489/.

Deci E., Koestner, R., and Ryan, R. (2001): "Extrinsic Rewards and Intrinsic Motivation in Education: Reconsidered Once Again", *Review of Education Research* 71, no. 1(Spring 2001): 14.

Deutschman, A. (2002): "The once and future Steve Jobs", October 11, 2000. Available at: http://www.salon.com/technology/books/2000/10/11/jobs_excerpt.

"Disagree and Commit: The Importance of disagreement in decision making", Hackernoon, January, 17 2019. Available at: https://hackernoon.com/disagree-and-commit-the-importance-of-disagreement-in-decision-making-b31d1b5f1bdc.

Duhigg, C. (2016): "What Google Learned From Its Quest to Build the Perfect Team", *The New York Times*, February 25, 2016. Available at: https://www.nytimes.com/2016/02/28/magazine/what-google-learned-from-its-quest-to-build-the-perfect-team.html.

Dunning, D., Heath, C., and Suls, J. "Flawed Self-Assessment: Implications for Health, Education, and the Workplace". *Psychol Sci*

Public Interest. 2004 Dec;5(3):69-106. doi: 10.1111/j.1529-1006.2004.00018.x. Epub 2004 Dec 1. PMID: 26158995.

Dunning, D. (2005): "Self-Insight: Roadblocks and Detours on the Path to Knowing Thyself". *Psychology Press*, New York. http://dx.doi.org/10.4324/9780203337998.

Dyer, J., Gregersen, H., and Christensen, C. (2008): "Entrepreuners Behaviours, Opportunity Recognition, and the Origins of Innovative Ventures", *Strategic Entrepreneurship Journal Strat.* J., 2: 317–338 (2008).

Eden, D. (1984): "Self-Fulfilling Prophecy as a Management Tool: Harnessing Pygmalion,", *Academy of Management Review* 9 (1984): 64-73.

Eden, D. y Shani, A. (1982). "Pygmalion goes to boot camp: Expectancy, leadership, and trainee performance" *Journal of Applied Psychology,* 67(2), 194–199. https://doi.org/10.1037/0021-9010.67.2.194.

Edmondson, A. C. (1999): "Psychological safety and learning behavior in work teams", *Administrative Science Quaterly*, 44, 350-383.

Edmondson, A. C. (2004): "Learning From Mistakes Is Easier Said Than Done. Group and Organizational Influences on the Detection and Correction of Human Error", *The Journal of Applied Behavioral Science*, Vol. 40 No. 1, March 2004.

Edwards, B. (2011): "The iPod: How Apple's legendary portable music player came to be", *Macworld*, October 23, 2011. Available at: https://www.macworld.com/article/1163181/the-birth-of-the-ipod.html.

Empson, R. (2012): "Silicon Valley, London, NYC," *TechCrunch* (2012). Available at: http://techcrunch.com/2012/04/10/startup-genome-compares-top-startup-hubs/.

"End of an Era: Google Executive Eric Schmidt to leave board", May 1, 2019, Brand&Leaders.com. Available at: https://www.brandsandleaders.com/2019/05/01/end-of-an-era-google-executive-eric-schmidt-to-leave-board/.

Eskridge, K. (2008): "They Watch Everything You Do,", *Humans at Work*, November 7, 2008. Available at: http://www.humansatwork.com.

Eisenhardt, K., and Schoonhoven, C. (1990): "Organizational Growth: Linking Founding Team, Strategy, Environment, and Growth Among U.S. Semiconductor Ventures, 1978-1988", *Administrative Science Quarterly* 35 (1990): 504-529.

Farber, D. (2014): "What Steve Jobs really meant when he said 'Good artists copy; great artists steal'", *CNET*, January 28, 2014. Available at: https://www.cnet.com/tech/tech-industry/what-steve-jobs-really-meant-when-he-said-good-artists-copy-great-artists-steal/.

Felps, W., Mitchell, T., and Byington, E. (2006): "How, When, And Why Bad Apple Spoil the Barrel: Negative Group Members and Dysfunctional Groups", *Research in Organizational Behavior*, Volume 27, 175-222 (2006).

Fildes, J. (2007): "Darwin's letters archive on web", BBC, May 16, 2007. Available at: http://news.bbc.co.uk/2/hi/science/nature/6657237.stm.

Fong, C. T. (2006): "The Effects of Emotional Ambivalence on Creativity", *The Academy of Management Journal*, Vol. 49, No. 5 (October 2006), pp. 1016-1030.

Gardner, N. (2006): "Emotionally ambivalent workers are more creative, innovative", University of Washington, October 5, 2006. Available at: http://www.washington.edu/news/2006/10/05/emotionally-ambivalent-workers-are-more-creative-innovative/.

Gaskins, R. (2012): "Viewpoint: How PowerPoint changed Microsoft and my life", BBC, July 31, 2012. Available at: www.bbc.com/news/technology.

Goldenberg, J., Mazursky, D., and Solomon, S. (1999): "Creative Sparks", *Science*, September 3, 1999, volumen 285, número 5433, pp. 1495-1496. Available at: https://www.science.org/doi/10.1126/science.285.5433.1495.

Gompers, P., Kovner, A., Lerner, J., and Scharfstein, D. (2006): "Skill vs. Luck in Entrepreneurship and Venture Capital: Evidence from Serial Entrepreneurs," NBER Working Papers 12592, *National Bureau of Economic Research*, Inc.

Govindarajan, V. (2010): "Innovation is not Creativity", Harvard Business Review, August 2, 2010. Available at: https://hbr.org/2010/08/innovation-is-not-creativity.

Grant, A. (2010): "Putting a Face to a Name: The Art of Motivating Employees", Knowledge at Wharton, University of Pennsylvania, February 17, 2010. Available at: https://knowledge.wharton.upenn.edu/article/putting-a-face-to-a-name-the-art-of-motivating employees/.

Grega, Al (2019): "A Brief History of the Mainframe World". Available at: https://community.ibm.com/community/user/ibmz-and-linuxone/blogs/destination-z1/2019/12/23/a-brief-history-of-the-mainframe.

Hansen, M. (2010): "IDEO CEO Tim Brown. T-Shaped Stars: The Backbone of IDEO's Collaborative Culture", Chief Excecutive, January 21, 2010. Available at: https://chiefexecutive.net/ideo-ceo-tim-brown-t-shaped-stars-the-backbone-of-ideoaes-collaborative-culture__trashed/.

Hargadon, A. (2010): "What is innovation", December 5, 2010. Available at: https://andrewhargadon.com/2010/12/05/what-is-innovation/.

Hatfield, E., Cacioppo, J., and Rapson, R. (1994): *Emotional Contagion*, Cambridge, UK: Cambridge University Press, 1994.

Helmer, J. (2012): "Harvard Grads' Startup Rewards Gym Rats, Penalizes Couch Potatoes", NBC News, May 27, 12. Available at: https://www.nbcnews.com/id/wbna47582216.

Hindo, B. (2007): "At 3M, A Struggle Between Efficiency And Creativity", June 11, 2007. Available at: https://www.effectuation.org/wp-content/uploads/2016/06/3m-struggle-between-efficiency-and-creativity.pdf.

Hirsch, J., and Hsu, T. (2014): "Elon Musk opens up Tesla patents; it 'isn't entirely altruistic", *Los Angeles Times,* June 12, 2014. Available at: https://www.latimes.com./business/autos/.

"How Elon Musk has missed his targets on delivering affordable cars", *Reuters*, March 1, 2023. Available at: https://www.reuters.com/business/autos-transportation/how-elon-musk-has-missed-his-targets-delivering-affordable-cars-2023-03-01/

"How to innovate the Silicon Valley way", *Deloitte University Press*. Available at: https://www2.deloitte.com/content/dam/insights/us/articles/tapping-into-silicon-valley-culture-of-innovation/DUP_3274_Silicon-Valley_MASTER.pdf.

IDEO, "Designing a School System from the Ground Up". Available at: https://www.ideo.com/case-study/designing-a-school-system-from-the-ground-up.

Schwab, K. (2017): "Ideo Studied Innovation In 100+ Companies–Here's What It Found", *Fast Company*, March 20, 2017. Available at: https://www.fastcompany.com/.

IDEO-Tools: "Creative Difference: A Customized Guide to a More Innovative and Adaptive Culure". Available at: https://www.ideo.com/post/creative-difference.

Isen, A., Daubman, K., and Nowicki, G. (1987): "Positive Affect Facilitates Creative Problem Solving". *Journal of Personality and Social Psychology,* 52(6), 1122–1131. https://doi.org/10.1037/0022-3514.52.6.1122.

Isen, A., Rosenzweig, A., and Young, M. (1991): "The Influence of Positive Affect on Clinical Problem Solving". *Medical Decision Making.* 1991;11(3):221-227. doi:10.1177/0272989X9101100313.

"Jeff Dyer on Innovation" (2017): Available at: https://www.linkedin.com/learning/jeff-dyer-on-innovation.

"Jeff Bezos explicó cómo su empresa espacial salvará a la humanidad" *Infobae*, April 20, 2018.

Karbo, K. (2019): "Jane Goodall, how a woman redefined mankind", *National Geographic*, January 18, 2019. Available at: https://www.nationalgeographic.com/culture/article/jane-goodall-book-excerpt-praise-difficult-women.

Keltner, D., Gruenfeld, D., and Anderson, C. (2003): "Power, approach, and inhibition". *Psychological Review,* 110(2), 265–284. https://doi.org/10.1037/0033-295X.110.2.265.

Kerr, S. (1995): "On the folly of rewarding A, while hoping for B", *Academy of Management Executive*, 1995, Vol. 9, No. 1.

Kirby, J., and Stewart, T. (2007): "The Institutional Yes", Harvard Business Review, October 2007. Available at: https://hbr.org/2007/10/the-institutional-yes.

Kirton, M. (1976). "Adaptors and innovators: A description and measure". *Journal of Applied Psychology,* 61(5), 622–629. https://doi.org/10.1037/0021-9010.61.5.622.

Krantz, M. (2022): "13 Firms Hoard $1 Trillion In Cash (We're Looking At You Big Tech)", *Investors Business Daily*, February 3, 2022. Available at: https://www.investors.com/etfs-and-funds/sectors/sp500-companies-stockpile-1-trillion-cash-investors-want-it/.

Krause, M. (2004): "El renacimiento del capitalismo emprendedor", Libertad digital, August 10, 2004. Available at: https://www.libertaddigital.com.

Lambert, F. (2022): "Tesla still dominates US electric car market, and it´s not even closs", *Electrek*, March 17, 2022. Available at: https://electrek.co/2022/03/17/tesla-still-dominates-us-electric-car-market/.

"La NASA quiere fabricar oxígeno a partir de dióxido de carbono en Marte", *La Nación*, Buenos Aires, August 24, 2017. Available at: https://www.lanacion.com.ar/sociedad/la-nasa-quiere-fabricar-oxigeno-a-partir-de-dioxido-de-carbono-en-marte-nid2056170/.

Lashinsky, A. (2011): "How Apple Works: Inside the World's Biggest Startup", *Fortune*, May 9, 2011. Available at: https://fortune.com/2011/05/09/inside-apple/.

Lasorda, T. Available at: https://www.brainyquote.com/quotes/tommy_lasorda_139448.

Leadership Foundry, "Do You Know How to RETAIN TALENT?. Available at: https://www.leadershipfoundry.com/retain-talent/.

Levy, S. (2007): "Google Goes Globe-Trotting", *Newsweek*, November 3, 2007. Available at: https://www.newsweek.com/google-goes-globe-trotting-96341. Livingston, J. (1969): "Pygmalion in Management", *Harvard Business Review* 47 (1969): 81-89.

Lopez, A., Esquivel, G., and Houtz, J. (1993): "The Creative Skills of Culturally and Linguistically Diverse Gifted Students", *Creativity Research Journal* 6 (1993): 401-412.

Ma, A. (2019): "Jeff Bezos wants floating colonies in space with weather like Maui all year long-here's what he thinks they'll look like" *Business Insider*, May 10, 2019. Available at: https://www.businessinsider.com./. Mark, G., Gonzalez, V. y Harris, J. (2005): "No Task Left Behind? Examining the Nature of Fragmented Work" (paper, CHI 2005, Portland, OR, abril 2-7, 2005), 113-120.

Mark, G., Gudith, D., and Klocke, U. (2008): "The Cost of Interrupted Work: More Speed and Stress", en *Proceedings of the Twenty-Sixth Annual SIGCHI Conference on Human Factors in Computing Systems* (New York: ACM, 2008), 107-110.

Martin, L.N., and Delgado, M.R. (2011): "The influence of emotion regulation on decision-making under risk". *J Cogn Neurosci*. 2011 Sep;23(9):2569-81. doi: 10.1162/jocn.2011.21618. Epub 2011 Jan 21. PMID: 21254801; PMCID: PMC3164848.

Messick, D., and Kramer, R. (2005): *The Psychology of Leadership: New Perspectives and Research*, Mahwah New Jersey, Lawrence Erlbaum Associates.

McBride, E. (2014): "Slam the Clam: Lesson From BP's Fast Growth", *Forbes*, October 31, 2014. Available at: https://www.forbes.com/sites/elizabethmacbride/2014/10/31/slam-the-clam-what-you-can-take-from-a-british-petroleum-slogan/Una clase con Huggy Rao.

Mediratta, B. (2007): "The Google Way: Give Engineers Room", *New York Times*, October 21, 2007. Available at: https://www.nytimes.com/2007/10/21/jobs/21pre.html.

"Microsoft's Kevin Scott & Kathleen Hogan discuss Bay Area presence & careers", *The Official Microsoft Blog*, February 28, 2019. Available at: https://blogs.microsoft.com/bayarea/2019/02/28/microsoft-growth-conference-kevin-scott-kathleen-hogan/

"Microsoft´s Downfall: Inside the Executive E-Mails and Cannibalisti Culture that Felled a Tech Giant", *Vanity Fair*, July, 3 2012. Available at: https://www.vanityfair.com/news.

Mintzberg, H. (1990): "The Manager´s Jobs: Folklore and Fact", Harvard Business Review, (March-April 1990). Available at: https://hbr.org/1990/03/the-managers-job-folklore-and-fact.

Mitsch, R. (1990): "Three Roads to Innovation", *Journal of Business Strategy*, 11, no. 5 (1990): 18-21.

Mossberg, W., and Swisher, K. (2019): "Steve Jobs and Bill Gates Face Off". Available at: https://www.youtube.com/watch?v=Sw8x7ASpRIY&t=1286s.

Mueller, W. (1962): "The Origins of the Basic Innovations Underlying DuPont´s Major Product and Process Innovations, 1920 to 1950", in *The Rate and Direction of Inventive Activity: Economic and Social Factors*, Princeton, National Bureau of Economics, 1962, pp. 323-358. Available at: https://www.nber.org/system/files/chapters/c2125/c2125.pdf.

Neighmond, P. (2014): "People Who Feel They Have A Purpose In Life Live Longer", NPR, July 28, 2014. Available at: https://www.npr.org/sections/healthshots/2014/07/28/334447274/people-who-feel-they-have-a-purpose-in-life-live-longer.

Nyberg, A. et al. (2009): "Managerial Leadership and Ischaemic Heart Disease Among Employees: The Swedish WOLF Study", *Occupational and Environmental Medicine* 66 (2009): 51-55.

O´Connor, G., and McDermott, C. (2004): "The Human Side of Radical Innovation", *Journal of Engineering Technology Management*, 21 (2004): 11-30.

Ortega y Gasset, J. (1983): *Obras completas* Tomo I (1902-1916), Glosas, De la crítica personal, Madrid: Revista de Occidente.

Ocean Tomo (2020): "Intangible Asset Market Value Study-Ocean Tomo". Available at: https://oceantomo.com/intangible-asset-market-value-study/. Updated to 2020.

Pandey, E. (2018): "How Barnes & Noble, the last big bookstore, fell to Amazon", *Axios*, October 7, 2018. Available at: https://www.axios.com/2018/10/04/barnes-and-noble-book-stores-sale-amazon-effect.

"Popular Play-Doh Turns 30 This Year", *Baltimore Sun*, October 7, 1985, 1B, 3B and www.yippeee.com y www.hasbro.com.

Rao H., Sutton, R. y Webb, A. (2008): "Innovation lessons from Pixar: An interview with Oscar-winning director Brad Bird", *McKinsey Quaterly*, April 2008. Available at: https://www.mckinsey.com.

Rinne, T., Steel, D., and Fairweather, J. (2012): "Hofstede and Shane Revisited: The Role of Power Distance and Individualism in National-Level Innovation Success", *Cross-Cultural Research 46 (2) 91-108*, Lincoln University, New Zeland, *SAGE Publications*.

Rinne, T., Steel, D., and Fairweather, J. (2012): "Hofstede and Shane Revisited: The Role of Power Distance and Individualism in National-Level Innovation Success", *Cross-Cultural Research 46 (2) 91-108, SAGE Publications*.

Rodgers, T.J. (2000): "Why Silicon Valley Should Not Normalize Relations With Washington D.C.", *Cato Institute*, September 4, 2000. Available at: https://www.cato.org/white-paper/why-silicon-valley-should-not-normalize-relations-washington-dc.

Rodriguez M., Juan "Leonardo da Vinci: ¿un Steve Jobs renacentista?", *Economía y negocios* on line, *El Mercurio*, June 3, 2018. Available at: http://www.economiaynegocios.cl/noticias/noticias.asp?id=474544.

Rosoff, M. (2011): "Andreessen and Horowitz Charges Employees $10 Per Minute If They´re Late To Meetings", *Business Insider*, March 1, 2011. Available at: https://www.businessinsider.com/andreessen-horowitz-adds-fourth-partner-2011-3.

Rosenthal, R., and Rubin, D. B. (1978): "Interpersonal Expectancy Effects: The First 345 Studies", *Behavioral and Brain Sciences* 3 (1978): 377-86.

Rosenthal, R., and Jacobson, L. (1968): *Pygmalion in the Classroom: Teacher Expectations and Pupils' Intellectual Development,* New York: Holt, Rinehart & Winston.

Rozovsky, J. (2015): "The five keys to a successful Google team", re Work, November 17, 2015. Available at: https://rework.withgoogle.com/blog/five-keys-to-a-successful-google-team/.

"Ruining it for the Rest of Us", *This American Life*, episode 370, December 19, 2008. Available at: https://www.thisamericanlife.org/370/ruining-it-for-the-rest-of-us.

Sahlman, W. (1997): "How to Make a Great Business Plan", Harvard Business Review (julio-agosto 1997) p. 101. Available at: https://hbr.org/1997/07/how-to-write-a-great-business-plan.

Salter, C. (2008): "Marissa Mayer's 9 Principles of Innovation", *FastCompany*, 2-19-2008. Available at: https://www.fastcompany.com/702926/marissa-mayers-9-principles-innovation.

Salvi, C., Bricolo, E., Kounios J., Bowden, E., and Beeman, M. "Insight solutions are correct more often than analytic solutions. Think Reason". 2016;22(4):443-460. doi: 10.1080/13546783.2016.1141798. Epub 2016 Feb 5. PMID: 27667960; PMCID: PMC5035115.

Sawyer, D. (1981): "Steve Jobs. Person of the Week", *ABC News*, January 29, 1981. Available at: http://abcnews.go.com/WN/abcs-world-news-diane-sayer-person-week steve/story?id=9699563&page=1.

Scott, S. (1992): "Why do some societies invent more than others?", *Journal of Business Venturing* 7, 29-46.

Scott, D. A., Viguerie, P., Schwartz, E., and Van Landeghem, J. (2018): "2018 Corporate Longevity Forecast: Creative Destruction is Accelerating", *Innosight*, February 6, 2018. Available at: https://www.innosight.com/insight/creative-destruction.

"Seis atributos innovadores que debe tener una organización para no desaparecer", *Infobae*, June 25, 2019. Available at: https//www.infobae.com/tendencias/talent-y-liderazgo.

Sellers, P. (2004): "P&G: Teaching An Old Dog New Tricks CEO A.G. Lafley has kicked up the good ideas at the stodgy Midwestern giant-and the company's growth too. Here's an inside look at how he's doing it." *CNN Money*, May 31, 2004. Available at: https://money.cnn.com/magazines/fortune/fortune_archive/2004/05/31/370714/index.htm.

Sharkey, J. (2010): "Reinventing the Suitcase by Adding the Wheel", *The New York Times*, October 4, 2010. Available at: https://www.nytimes.com/2010/10/05/business/05road.html.

Silicon Valley Chamber of Commerce. Available at: https://www.svcentralchamber.com/we-are-silicon-valley/.

"Silicon Valley 2022 Index". Available at: https://jointventure.org/images/stories/pdf/index2022.pdf. p.47.

Simonton, D. K. (1995). "Foresight in insight? A Darwinian answer". In R. J. Sternberg & J. E. Davidson (Eds.), *The nature of insight* (pp. 465–494). The MIT Press.

Sinek, S. "How Great Leaders Inspire Action". Available at: https://www.ted.com/talks/simon_sinek_how_great_leaders_inspire_action?language=en.

Snell, J. (2011): "Steve Jobs: Making a dent in the universe", *Macworld*, October 6, 2011. Available at: https://www.macworld.com/article/214642/steve-jobs-making-a-dent-in-the-universe.html.

Statista. Available at: https://www.statista.com/statistics/277501/venture-capital-amount-invested-in-the-united-states-since-1995/.

Stanford Nobel Laureates. Available at: https://news.stanford.edu/nobel/#:~:text=Stanford%20University%20is%20home%20to%2020%20living%20Nobel%20laureates.

"Stanford Facts 2015". Available at: http://facts.stanford.edu/pdf/StanfordFacts_2015.pdf).

Mossberg, W., and Swisher, K. "Steve Jobs talks about managing people". Available at: https://www.youtube.com/watch?v=f60dheI4ARg.

Steve, Jobs: speech at Stanford, June 12, 2005. Available at: https://news.stanford.edu/2005/06/14/jobs-061505/.

Stevens, G., and Burley, J. (1997): "3000 Raw Ideas=1 Commercialized Success!", *Research Technology Management,* Vol. 40, No. 3 (May-June 1997), pp. 16-27. Published By: Taylor & Francis, Ltd.

Sutton, R. (2010): "It´s Up to You to Start a Good Fight", Harvard Business Review, August 3, 2010. Available at: https://hbr.org/2010/08/its-up-to-you-to-start-a-good.

Sutton, R. "Some Bosses Live in a Fool´s Paradise", Harvard Business Review, June 3, 2010. Available at: https://hbr.org/2010/06/some-bosses-live-in-a-fools-pa.

Sutton, R. "Fight Like You're Right, Listen Like You're Wrong and Other Keys to Great Management", *First Round Review,* Management. Available at: https://firstround.com/review/Fight-Like-Youre-Right-Listen-Like-Youre-Wrong-and-Other-Keys-to-Great-Management/.

Sutton, R. (2014): "Why Big Teams Suck: Seven (Plus or Minus Two) is the Magical Number Once Again". Available at: https://bobsutton.typepad.com/my_weblog/2014/03/why-big-teams-suck-seven-plus-or-minus-two-is-the-magical-number-once-again.html.

Sutton, R. (2010): "The Delicate Art of Being Perfectly Assertive", Harvard Business Review, June 28, 2010. Available at: https://hbr.org/2010/06/the-delicate-art-of-being-perf.

Sutton, R. (2010): "Managing yourself: the Boss as a Human Shield", Harvard Business Review, September 2010. Available at: https://hbr.org/2010/09/managing-yourself-the-boss-as-human-shield.

Sutton, R. (2011): "Pixar Lore: The Day Our Bosses Saved Our Jobs", Harvard Business Review, January 10, 2011. Available at: https://hbr.org/2011/01/pixar-lore-the-day-our-bosses.

Sutton, R. (2012): "Dysfunctional Internal Competition at Microsoft: we've seen the enemy, and it is us!", July 6, 2012. Available at: https://bobsutton.typepad.com/my_weblog/2012/07/dysfunctional-internal-competition-at-microsoft-weve-seen-the-enemy-and-it-is-us.html.

Sydell, L. (2011): "Apple Visionary Steve Jobs Dies at 56", October 5, 2011. Available at: https://www.npr.org/2011/10/05/123826622/apple-visionary-steve-jobs-dies-at-56.

Tang, S. y Aycan, D. "How to Set the Conditions for Innovation", IDEO, July 6, 2018. Available at: https://www.ideo.com/search?q=Creative%20Difference.

Taylor, M. Z., and Wilson, S. (2012): "Does culture still matter?: The effects of individualism on national innovation rates", *Journal of Business Venturing* 27 (2012), 234-247.

Tett, G. (2015): "Why the silo effect makes us stupid", *Financial Review*, August 28, 2015. Available at: https://www.afr.com/life-and-luxury/arts-and-culture/the--big-walkman-switchoff-how-silos-stifle-progress-in-the-digital-age-20150824-gj64kk.

"This is the Way Google & IDEO Foster Creativity". IDEO University. Available at: https://www.ideou.com/blogs/inspiration/how-google-fosters-creativity-innovation.

"The Slow Death of Design", 16-11-2023, Design Shangai: Stories, Available at: https://design.shangai/stories.

Tiger, L. (1970): "Dominance in Human Societies", *Annual Review of Ecology and Systematics* Vo. 1 (1970): 298.

"Triumph of the Nerds 1995". Available at: https://allaboutstevejobs.com/videos/misc/triumph_of_the_nerds_interview_1995.

Tucker, A. L., and Edmondson, A.C. (2003): "Why hospitals don´t learn from failures: Organizational and psychological dynamics that inhibit system change", *California Management Review*, 45, 55-72.

Usborne, D. (2012): "The moment it all went wrong for Kodak", *The Independent*, January 20, 2012. Available at: https://www.independet.co.uk/news/business/analysis-and-features.

Wadhwa, V. et al. (2012): "Then and Now: America's New Immigrant Entrepreneurs, Part VII", Ewing Marion Kauffman Foundation Research Paper. Stanford Public Law Working Paper No. 2159875. Rock Center for Corporate Governance at Stanford University Working Paper No. 127 Oct 2012. Available at: https://www.kauffman.org/.

Vohs, K., Baumeister, R., Bratslavsky, E., and Finkenauer, C. (2001): "Bad is Stronger Than Good", *Review of General Psychology*, 2001, Vol. 5, No. 4, 323-370.

Vohs, K., Mead, N., and Goode, M. (2006): "The Psychological Consequences of Money", *Science*, Vol. 314, No. 5802, (November 17, 2006), pp. 1154-1156.

Weber, R. et al. (2001): "The Illusion of Leadership: Misattribution of Cause in Coordination Games", *Organization Science* 12, (2001): 582-598.

Weick, K. E. (1984): "Small Wins: Redefining the Scale of Social Problems", *American Psychologist* 39 (1984): 40-49.

Weintraub, S. (2013): "IDEO founder David Kelley talks design, Steve Jobs, cancer, and the importance of empathy", *9to5Mac*, January 6, 2013. Available at: https://9to5mac.com/2013/01/06/ideo-founder-david-kelley-talks-design-steve-jobs-cancer-and-the-importance-of-empathy/.

"Why Americans Should Embrace Immigration". Available at: https://citizenpath.com/immigrantcontributions/#:~:text=Immigrant%20founders%20started%2052%20percent,impact%20of%20the%20recognizable%20brands.

Williams, J. (1990): "The Rise of Silicon Valley", Invention & Technology, Spring/Summer 1990. Available at: https://www.academia.edu/438975.

Wolf, G. (1996): "Steve Jobs: The Next Insanely Great Thing", *Wired*, February 1, 1996. Available at: https://www.wired.com/1996/02/jobs-2/.

"Wondered why toothbrushes for kids are really fat?" NTRPD, *Medium*, Available at: https://medium.com/@NTRPD/wondered-why-toothbrushes-for-kids-arereally-fat-6a586fe12db.

Woolley, A. et al. (2010): "Evidence for a Collective Intelligence Factor in the Performance of Human Groups", *Science*, September 30, 2010, Vol 330, Issue 6004, pp. 686-688. DOI: 10.1126/science.1193147. Available at: https://www.science.org/doi/10.1126/science.1193147.

Yang, A. (2007): "Waiter, I'm at Your Mercy", *The New York Times*, July 22, 2007. Available at: https://www.nytimes.com/2007/07/22/travel/22surfacing.html.

Yamashita, K. (IDEO): *From Superpowers to Great Teams* en IDEO University. Available at: https://www.ideou.com/products/leading-for-creativity.

Zenger, J., Folkman, J., and Edinger, S. (2009): "How Extraordinary Leaders Double Profits", *Chief Learning Officer*, July 2009.

Ziegler, M. (2021): "7 Famous Quotes You Definitely Didn't Know Were From Women", *Forbes*, September 1, 2014. Available at: https://www.forbes.com/sites/maseenaziegler/2014/09/01/how-we-all-got-it-wrong-women-were-behind-these-7-famously-inspiring-quotes/.

"8 Steve Jobs Quotes Every Entrepreneur Should Live By", May 6, 2005. Available at: https://www.businessnewsdaily.com/7962-steve-jobs-quotes.html.

"201 Amazing Steve Jobs Quotes (That Will Motivate You)". Available at: http://wisdomquotes.com/steve-jobs-quotes/.

Footnotes

[1] Boltgroup (2016). "You Manage Things; You Lead People", *Boltgroup*, August 16, 2016. Available at: https://boltgroup.com/manage-things-lead-people/.

[2] Cornell University, INSEAD, and WIPO (2015): *The Global Innovation Index 2015: Effective Innovation Policies for Development*, Fontainebleau, Ithaca, and Geneva, p. 41. Grega, A. (2019). "A Brief History of the Mainframe World". Available at: https://community.ibm.com/community/user/ibmz-and-linuxone/blogs/destination-z1/2019/12/23/a-brief-history-of-the-mainframe.

[3] Oppenheimer, A. (2014). Oppenheimer, A. *¡Crear o Morir!,* Buenos Aires: Sudamericana, p. 60.

[4] Christensen, C. M. (1997). *The Innovator's Dilemma: When New Technologies Cause Great Firms to Fail,* Boston: Harvard Business School Press, p. 109.

[5] Isaacson, W. (2014). *Los innovadores,* Buenos Aires: Debate, p. 174.

[6] Christensen, C. M. (1997). *The Innovator's Dilemma*...ob. cit., p. xv.

[7] Isaacson, W. (2014). *Los innovadores*...ob. cit., p. 277 (free translation from Spanish version of Isaacson´s book into English).

[8] Williams, J. (1990). "The Rise of Silicon Valley", *Invention & Technology*, Spring/Summer 1990. Available at: https://www.academia.edu/438975.

[9] Isaacson, W. (2014). *Los innovadores*...ob. cit., p. 218.

[10] Ibidem, p. 217.

[11] Ibidem, p. 217.

[12] Ibidem, p. 523.

[13] Clark Scott, D. (2011). "Robert Noyce: Why Steve Jobs idolized Noyce", *The Christian Science Monitor,* December 12, 2011.

[14] Mossberg, W., and Swisher, K. "Steve Jobs talks about managing people". Available at: https://www.youtube.com/watch?v=f60dheI4ARg.

[15] Berlin, L. (2005). *The Man behind the Microchip: Robert Noyce and the Invention of Silicon Valley,* New York: Oxford University Press, p. 207.

[16] Byers, T., Dorf, R., and Nelson, A. (2015). *Technology Ventures: From Idea To Enterprise,* New York: McGraw Hill, p. 262. Bartlett, C. and Ghoshal, S. (2002): "Building Competitive Advange through People". *MIT Sloan Management Review* (Winter), pp. 34-41.

[17] Rodgers, T.J. (2000). "Why Silicon Valley Should Not Normalize Relations With Washington D.C.", *Cato Institute*, September 4, 2000. p. 2.

[18] Silicon Valley Chamber of Commerce. Available at: https://www.svcentralchamber.com/we-are-silicon-valley/.

[19] "How to innovate the Silicon Valley way", Deloitte University Press. Available at: https://www2.deloitte.com/content/dam/insights/us/articles/tapping-into-silicon-valley-culture-of-innovation/DUP_3274_Silicon-Valley_MASTER.pdf.

[20] "Why Americans Should Embrace Immigration". Available at: https://citizenpath.com/immigrantcontributions/#:~:text=Immigrant%20founders%20started%2052%20percent,impact%20of%20the%20recognizable%20brands. Wadhwa et al. (2012). "Then and Now: America's New Immigrant Entrepreneurs, Part VII", Ewing Marion Kauffman Foundation Research Paper. Stanford Public Law Working Paper No. 2159875. Rock Center for Corporate Governance at Stanford University Working Paper No. 127 Oct. 2012.

[21] "Best Practices in State and Regional Innovation Initiatives: Competing in the 21st Century", V. Annex AStanford and Silicon Valley, *National Academy of Sciences,* 2013. Available at: https://www.ncbi.nlm.nih.gov/books/NBK158815/. Stanford Nobel Laureates. Available at: https://news.stanford.edu/nobel/#:~:text=Stanford%20University%20is%20home%20to%2020%20living%20Nobel%20laureates.

[22] Ibidem.

[23] "Stanford Facts 2015". Available at: http://facts.stanford.edu/pdf/StanfordFacts_2015.pdf. pp. 1-46.

[24] *Index of Silicon Valley 2022.* Available at: https://jointventure.org/images/stories/pdf/index2022.pdf. p.47.

[25] Rodriguez, M., J. (2018). "Leonardo da Vinci: ¿un Steve Jobs renacentista?", *Economía y negocios,* June 3, 2018.

[26] *Index of Silicon Valley 2022.* Available at: https://jointventure.org/images/stories/pdf/index2022.pdf. p.47.

[27] "Silicon Valley, London, NYC," *TechCrunch* (2012). Available at: http://techcrunch.com/2012/04/10/startup-genome-compares-top-startup-hubs/.

[28] *Index of Silicon Valley 2022,* Available at: https://jointventure.org/images/stories/pdf/index2022.pdf. p.47.

[29] Alaban, L. (2021). "San Jose Legends: John Sobrato's generosity is everywhere", *San José Spotlight,* June 27, 2021. Available at: https://sanjosespotlight.com/san-jose-legends-john-sobratos-generosity-is-everywhere/.

[30] Ziegler, M. (2021). "7 Famous Quotes You Definitely Didn't Know Were From Women", *Forbes,* September 1, 2014.

[31] Conversation between a friend of mine and Bill Gates (an "elevator pitch").

[32] Usborne, D. (2012). "The moment it all went wrong for Kodak", *The Independent*, January 20, 2012. Available at: https://www.independet.co.uk/news/business/analysis-and-features.

[33] Govindarajan, V. (2010). "Innovation is not Creativity", August 2, 2010, *Harvard Business Review* (HBR).

[34] Byers T., Dorf, R., and Nelson, A. (2015). *Technology Ventures: From Idea To Enterprise*, New York: McGraw Hill, p. 465.

[35] "8 Steve Jobs Quotes Every Entrepreneur Should Live By", May 6, 2005. Available at: https://www.businessnewsdaily.com/7962-steve-jobs-quotes.html.

[36] "Arthur Rock, MBA 1951", Harvard Business Review. Available at: https://entrepreneurship.hbs.edu/founders/Pages/profile.aspx?num=24. Sahlman, W. (1997). "How to Make a Great Business Plan", Harvard Business Review (July-August 1997) p. 101.

[37] Hargadon, A. (2010). "What is innovation", December 5, 2010. Available at: https://andrewhargadon.com/2010/12/05/what-is-innovation/.

[38] Sharkey, J. (2010). "Reinventing the Suitcase by Adding the Wheel", *The New York Times*, October 4, 2010.

[39] Sala-i-Martin, X. (2017). *Economía en colores*, Barcelona: Penguin Random House, p. 54.

[40] "Popular Play-Doh Turns 30 This Year", *Baltimore Sun*, Octber 7, 1985, 1B, 3B and www.yippeee.com y www.hasbro.com.

[41] Sutton, R. (2002). *Weird Ideas That Work*, New York: Free Press, p. 25.

[42] Hargadon, A. (2003). *How Breakthroughs Happen: The Surprising Truth About How Companies Innovate*, Boston: Harvard Business School Press, p. 137.

[43] Reid, R. (1997). *Architects of the Web: 1,000 Days that Built the Future of Business*, New York: Wiley, p. 113.

44 Segaller, S. (1998). *Nerds 2.0.1.: A Brief History of the Internet*, New York: TV Books.

45 Hargadon, A. (2003). *How Breakthroughs Happen: The Surprising Truth About How Companies Innovate*...ob. cit., p. 33. *A History of Modern Computing*, Cambridge: MIT Press, 2002, p. 234.

46 Dyer J., Gregersen, H., and Christensen, C. (2015). *The Innovator's DNA: Mastering the Five Skills of Disruptive Innovators*...ob. cit., p. 178.

47 Isaacson, W. (2014). *Los innovadores*...ob. cit. pp. 402-403.

48 Farber, D. (2014). "What Steve Jobs really meant when he said 'Good artists copy; great artists steal'", CNET, January 28, 2014.

49 Hargadon, A. (2003). *How Breakthroughs Happen: The Surprising Truth About How Companies Innovate*...ob. cit., p. 43. Hounshell, D. (1984). *From the American System to Mass Production, 1800-1932: The Development of Manufacturing Technology in the United States*, vol. 4, *Studies of Industry and Society*, Baltimore: Johns Hopkins University Press, p.241.

50 Hargadon, A. (2003). *How Breakthroughs Happen: The Surprising Truth About How Companies Innovate*...ob. cit., p. 121.

51 Ibidem, p. 76.

52 Ibidem, p. 36.

53 Gordon, J. S. (2001). *The Business of America: Tales from the Marketplace- American Enterprise from the Settling of New England to the Breakup of AT&T*, New York: Walker & Company.

54 Rabinow, P. (1996). *Making PCR: A Story of Biotechnology*, Chicago: University of Chicago Press, pp. 6-7.

55 Simonton, D.K. (1996). "Foresight in Insight? A Darwinian Answer", *The Nature of Insight*, ed. Sternberg R. J. and Davidson, J. E., Cambridge: MIT Press, p. 468.

⁵⁶ Johansson, F. (2004). *The Medici Effect*, Boston: Harvard Business School Publishing, p. 101.

⁵⁷ Sydell, L. (2011). "Apple Visionary Steve Jobs Dies at 56", October 5, 2011. Available at: https://www.npr.org/2011/10/05/123826622/apple-visionary-steve-jobs-dies-at-56.

⁵⁸ Gallo, C. (2011). *The Innovation Secrets of Steve Jobs*, New York: McGraw-Hill.

⁵⁹ Johansson, F. (2004). *The Medici Effect*...ob. cit., pp. 26-27.

⁶⁰ Ibidem, p. 77.

⁶¹ Ibidem, pp. 23-24.

⁶² Johansson, F. (2004). *The Medici Effect*...ob. cit., p. 47. Campbell, D., "Blind Variation and Selective Retention in Creative Thought as in Other Knowledge Processes", *Psychological Review* 67, no.6 (1960): 380-400. Simonton, D. K. (1999). *Origins of Genius*, New York: Oxford University Press. Lopez, A.J., Esquivel, G. B., and Houtz, J.C. (1993). "The Creative Skills of Culturally and Linguistically Diverse Gifted Students", *Creativity Research Journal* 6 (1993): 401-412. Carringer, D.C. (1974). "Creative Thinking Abilities in Mexican Youth", *Journal of Cross-Cultural Psychology* 5 (1974): 492-504.

⁶³ Isaacson, W. (2014). *Los innovadores*...ob. cit., pp. 523-524.

⁶⁴ Mass, P. (1999). *The Terrible Hours: The Man Behind the Greatest Submarine Rescue in History*, New York: HarperCollins, p. 65. Sutton, R. *Weird Ideas That Work*...ob. cit., p. 116.

⁶⁵ Yang, A. (2007). "Waiter, I'm at Your Mercy", *The New York Times*, July 22.

⁶⁶ "Harvard grads turn gym business model on its head; fitness plan members pay more if they don't work out", *The Boston Globe*, January 24, 2011. Helmer, J. (2012). "Harvard Grads' Startup Rewards Gym Rats, Penalizes Couch Potatoes", NBC News, May 27, 2012. Available at: https://www.nbcnews.com/id/wbna47582216.

⁶⁷ Sutton, R. (2002). *Weird Ideas That Work*...ob. cit., p. 7.

[68] Ibidem, p. 5.

[69] Ibidem, p. 10.

[70] Stevens, G., and Burley, J. (1997). "3000 Raw Ideas=1 Commercialized Success!", *Research Technology Management*, 40,3.

[71] Wentz, R. C. (2012). *The Innovation Machine*: Germany, Amazon, p.141.

[72] Hindo, B. (2007). "At 3M, A Struggle Between Efficiency And Creativity", June 11, 2007. Available at: https://www.effectuation.org/wp-content/uploads/2016/06/3m-struggle-between-efficiency-and-creativity.pdf. Dyer J., Gregersen H. and Christensen C. M. *The Innovator's DNA: Mastering the Five Skills of Disruptive Innovators*, Boston: Harvard Business Review Press, 2011, p. 139.

[73] Johansson, F. (2004). *The Medici Effect*...ob. cit., p. 91.

[74] Michalko, M. (2001). *Craking Creativity*, Berkeley: Ten Speed Press, 2001.

[75] Simonton, D. K. *Origins of Genius: Darwinian Perpectives on Creativity*...ob. cit.

[76] Sawyer, D. (1981). "Steve Jobs. Person of the Week", ABC News, January 29, 1981. Available at: http://abcnews.go.com/WN/abcs-world-news-diane-sayer-person-week steve/story?id=9699563&page=1.

[77] Gompers P., Kovner, A., Lerner, J., and Scharfstein D. S. (2006). "Skill Versus Luck in Entrepreneurship", working paper 12592, National Bureau of Economic Research, 2006.

[78] Tellis, G. (2013). *Unrelenting Innovation, How to Build a Culture for Market Dominance*. San Francisco: Wiley & Sons, p. 144. O´Connor, G., and McDermott, C. (2004). "The Human Side of Radical Innovation", *Journal of Engineering Technology Management*, 21 (2004): 11-30.

[79] Bachrach, E. (2012). *AgilMente*, Buenos Aires: Sudamericana.

[80] Amabile, T., Hadley, C., and Kramer, S. (2002). "Creativity Under the Gun", Harvard Business Review, August, 2002.

[81] Johansson, F. (2004). *The Medici Effect*...ob. cit., pp. 184-185. Bruno, L. (2002). "Putting Quiks to Work", *Red Herring*, July 3, 2002.

[82] Bachrach, E., (2012). *AgilMente*...ob. cit., p. 134. Salvi, S., Bricolo, E., Kounios, J., Bowden, E., and Beeman, M. (2016). "Insight solutions are correct more often than analytic solutions", p. 443-460, February 5, 2016. Available at: https://doi.org/10.1080/13546783.2016.1141798.

[83] Hargadon, A. (2003). *How Breakthroughs Happen: The Surprising Truth About How Companies Innovate*...ob. cit., p. 78.

[84] Ibidem, p. 51.

[85] "La NASA quiere fabricar oxígeno a partir de dióxido de carbono en Marte", *La Nación*, Buenos Aires, August 24, 2017.

[86] Dyer, J., Gregersen, H., and Christensen, C. M. (2011). *The Innovator's DNA: Mastering the Five Skills of Disruptive Innovators*...ob. cit., p. 136.

[87] Byers, T. Dorf, R., and Nelson, A. (2015). *Technology Ventures: From Idea To Enterprise*...ob. cit. p. 409.

[88] Krause, M. (2004). "El renacimiento del capitalismo emprendedor", Libertad digital, August 10, 2004. Available at: https://www.libertaddigital.com.

[89] Rogers, S. (2002). *The Entrepreneur's Guide to Finance and Business*. McGraw Hill, p. 42.

[90] Byers, T., Dorf, R., and Nelson, A. (2015). *Technology Ventures: From Idea To Enterprise*...ob. cit. p. 8.

[91] Ibidem, p. 13.

[92] Ibidem, p. 246.

[93] Ocean Tomo (2020). "Intangible Asset Market Value Study - Ocean Tomo". Available at: https://oceantomo.com/intangible-asset-market-value-study/. Updated to 2020. Byers, T., Dorf, R., and Nelson, A. (2015). *Technology Ventures: From Idea To Enterprise* ...ob. cit., p. 280.

[94] Byers, T., Dorf, R., and Nelson, A. (2015). *Technology Ventures: From Idea To Enterprise*...ob. cit., p. 18.

[95] Gupta, P. (2007). *Business Innovation in the 21 Century*, South Carolina: BookSurge, LLC, An Amazon Company, 2007, pp. 34-35.

[96] del Bono, T. (2003). "La fuga de cerebros pone en riesgo el futuro", *La Nación*, Buenos Aires, November 12, 2003.

[97] Isaacson, W. (2014). *Los innovadores*...ob. cit. p. 344. Baer, D. (2013). "The Biggest Idea Bill Gates Ever Had", *Fast Company*, 10-11-2013.

[98] Tellis, G. (2013). *Unrelenting Innovation, How to Build a Culture for Market Dominance*...ob. cit., pp.92-98.

[99] Byers, T., Dorf, R., and Nelson A. (2015). *Technology Ventures: From Idea To Enterprise*...ob. cit., p. 403-410.

[100] Ibidem, p. 13.

[101] Souza, C. (2014). "More money, more problems: Open English, CEO Andrés Moreno Talks Funding", Tech Cocktail Miami, May 5, de 2014. Available at: en http://tech.co/andres-moreno-funding-2014-2015.

[102] Statista. Available at: https://www.statista.com/statistics/277501/venture-capital-amount-invested-in-the-united-states-since-1995/.

[103] Dyer, J., Gregersen, H., and Christensen C. (2008). "Entrepreuners Behaviours, Opportunity Recognition, and the Origins of Innovative Ventures", *Strategic Entrepreneurship Journal Strat. J.*, 2: 317–338 (2008).

[104] Wolf, G. (1997). "Steve Jobs: The Next Insanely Great Thing", *Wired*, February 1, 1997.

[105] Dyer, J., Gregersen, H., and Christensen, C. (2011). *The Innovator's DNA: Mastering the Five Skills of Disruptive Innovators*...ob. cit., p. 54.

[106] Ibidem, p. 3.

[107] Ibidem, p. 25.

[108] Ibidem, p. 25.

[109] Dyer, J., Gregersen, H., and Christensen, C. (2008). "Entrepreuners Behaviours, Opportunity Recognition, and the Origins of Innovative Ventures", *Strategic Entrepreneurship Journal Strat. J.*, 2: 317–338 (2008). Eadicicco, L. (2020). "Laurene Powell Jobs says people have been misinterpreting one of Steve Jobs' most famous quotes for years", *Business Insider*, February 28, 2020.

[110] Dyer J., Gregersen H., and Christensen C. (2008). "Entrepreuners Behaviours, Opportunity Recognition, and the Origins of Innovative Ventures", *Strategic Entrepreneurship Journal* J., 2: 317–338 (2008).

[111] Spitzer, Q., and Evans, R. (1997). *Heads You Win: How the Best Companies Think*, New York: Simon and Schuster, 1997, p. 41. Dyer, J., Gregersen, H. and Christensen, C. (2011). *The Innovator's DNA: Mastering the Five Skills of Disruptive Innovators*…ob. cit., p. 68.

[112] Gallo, C. (2011). *The Innovation Secrets of Steve Jobs*, New York: McGraw-Hill, 2011, p. 96. Dyer J., Gregersen, H., and Christensen, C. (2011). *The Innovator's DNA: Mastering the Five Skills of Disruptive Innovators*…ob. cit., p. 201.

[113] Dyer J., Gregersen, H., and Christensen, C. (2011). *The Innovator's DNA: Mastering the Five Skills of Disruptive Innovators*…ob. cit., p. 65.

[114] Dyer J., Gregersen, H., and Christensen, C. (2011). *The Innovator's DNA: Mastering the Five Skills of Disruptive Innovators*…ob. cit., p. 90.

[115] Ibidem, p. 42.

[116] Ortega y Gasset, J. (1983). *Obras completas* Tomo I (1902-1916), Glosas, De la crítica personal, Madrid: Revista de Occidente, p. 15.

[117] "This is the Way Google & IDEO Foster Creativity". IDEO University. Available at: https://www.ideou.com/blogs/inspiration/how-google-fosters-creativity-innovation.

[118] "This is the Way Google & IDEO Foster Creativity". IDEO University. Available at: https://www.ideou.com/blogs/inspiration/how-google-fosters-creativity-innovation.

[119] Dyer J., Gregersen, H., and Christensen C. (2011). *The Innovator's DNA: Mastering the Five Skills of Disruptive Innovators*...ob. cit., p. 74.

[120] Shultz, H., and Yang, D. (1997). *Pour Your Heart Into It: How Starbucks Built a Company One Cup at a Time*, New York: Hyperion, 1997, pp. 51-52.

[121] Dyer J., Gregersen, H., and Christensen C. (2011). *The Innovator's DNA: Mastering the Five Skills of Disruptive Innovators*...ob. cit., p. 142. Carpenter M., Sanders, G., and Gregersen, H. (2001). "Building Human Capital: The Impact of International Assignment Experience on CEO Pay and Multinational Firm Performance", *Academy of Management Journal* 44, no. 3 (2001): 493-512.

[122] Dyer J., Gregersen, H., and Christensen, C. (2011). *The Innovator's DNA: Mastering the Five Skills of Disruptive Innovators*...ob. cit., p. 134.

[123] Ibidem, p. 95.

[124] Kelley, T. (2005). *The Art of Innovation*, New York: Doubleday, 2005, p. 16.

[125] Dyer J., Gregersen, H., and Christensen C. (2011). *The Innovator's DNA: Mastering the Five Skills of Disruptive Innovators*...ob. cit., p. 100. "Wondered why toothbrushes for kids are really fat?". Available at: https://medium.com/@NTRPD/wondered-why-toothbrushes-for-kids-arereally-fat-6a586fe12db.

[126] Dyer J., Gregersen, H., and Christensen C. (2011). *The Innovator's DNA: Mastering the Five Skills of Disruptive Innovators*...ob. cit., p. 136. On the process of *working backwards*: "Jeff Dyer on Innovation". Available at: https://www.linkedin.com/learning/jeff-dyer-on-innovation.

[127] Dyer J., Gregersen, H., and Christensen, C. (2011). *The Innovator's DNA: Mastering the Five Skills of Disruptive Innovators*...ob. cit., p. 135.

[128] "Jeff Bezos explicó cómo su empresa espacial salvará a la humanidad" *Infobae*, April 20, 2018. "Jeff Bezos wants floating colonies in space with weather like Maui all year long-here's what he thinks they'll look like" *Business Insider*, May 10, 2019.

[129] Dyer J., Gregersen, H., and Christensen, C. (2011). *The Innovator's DNA: Mastering the Five Skills of Disruptive Innovators*...ob. cit., p. 136.

[130] Ibidem, p. 144.

[131] Ibidem, p. 144.

[132] "Jeff Dyer on Innovation". Available at: https://www.linkedin.com/learning/jeff-dyer-on-innovation.

[133] Dyer, J., Gregersen, H., and Christensen, C. (2011). *The Innovator's DNA: Mastering the Five Skills of Disruptive Innovators*...ob. cit., p. 24.

[134] Ibidem, p. 116.

[135] Ibidem, p. 117.

[136] Ibidem, pp. 205-206.

[137] "The Origins of the Basic Innovations Underlying DuPont´s Major Product and Process Innovations, 1920 to 1950", in *The Rate and Direction of Inventive Activity: Economic and Social Factors*, Princeton: National Bureau of Economics, 1962, pp. 323-358.

[138] Wentz, R.C. (2012). *The Innovation Machine*...ob. cit., p.312.

[139] Kelley, T., and Kelley, D. (2013). *Creative Confidence*, New York: Random House, 2013, p. 3.

[140] Dyer, J., Gregersen, H., and Christensen C. (2011). *The Innovator's DNA: Mastering the Five Skills of Disruptive Innovators*...ob. cit., p. 80. Deutschman, A. (2000). "The once and future Steve Jobs", October 11, 2000. Available at: http://www.salon.com/technology/books/2000/10/11/jobs_excerpt.

[141] "Turning Limitations into Innovations", *BusinessWeek*, February 1, 2006. Dyer, J., Gregersen, H., and Christensen, C. M. (2011). *The Innovator's DNA: Mastering the Five Skills of Disruptive Innovators*...ob. cit., p. 78.

[142] Goldenberg, J., Mazursky, D., and Solomon, S. (1999). "Creative Sparks", *Science*, September 3, 1999, Vol. 285, Nbr. 5433, pp. 1495-1496.

[143] Dyer, J., Gregersen, H., and Christensen, C. (2008). "Entrepreuners Behaviours, Opportunity Recognition, and the Origins of Innovative Ventures", *Strategic Entrepreneurship Journal* J., 2: 317–338 (2008).

[144] Dyer, J., Gregersen, H., and Christensen, C. (2011). *The Innovator's DNA: Mastering the Five Skills of Disruptive Innovators*...ob. cit., pp. 195-196.

[145] Levy, S. (2007). "Google Goes Globe-Trotting", *Newsweek*, November 12, 2007: 62-64.

[146] Gallo, C. (2011). *The Innovation Secrets of Steve Jobs*, New York: McGraw-Hill, 2011. Dyer J., Gregersen, H., and Christensen, C. (2011). *The Innovator's DNA: Mastering the Five Skills of Disruptive Innovators*...ob. cit., p. 197.

[147] Dyer, J., Gregersen, H., and Christensen, C. (2011). *The Innovator's DNA: Mastering the Five Skills of Disruptive Innovators*...ob. cit., p. 218.

[148] Levy, S. (2006). *The Perfect Thing: How the iPod Shuffles Commerce, Culture, and Coolness*, New York: Simon & Schuster, 2006, p. 118. Dyer J., Gregersen, H. ,and Christensen, C. (2011). *The Innovator's DNA: Mastering the Five Skills of Disruptive Innovators*...ob. cit., p. 217.

[149] Dyer J., Gregersen, H., and Christensen, C. (2011). *The Innovator's DNA: Mastering the Five Skills of Disruptive Innovators*...ob. cit., p. 218.

[150] Ibidem, p. 165-166.

[151] Answers.com, "Jeff Bezos", May 2003. Available at: http://www.answers.com/topic/jeff bezos.

[152] Mitsch, R. (1990). "Three Roads to Innovation", *Journal of Business Strategy*, 11, no. 5 (1990): 18-21.

[153] *A Century of Innovation, The 3M Story*, International Standard Book, 2002, p. 224. Available at: http://multimedia.3m.com.

[154] Pink, D. (2009). *Drive, The Surprising Truth About What Motivates Us,* New York: Riverhead Book, 2009, p. 94.

[155] Ibidem, p. 94.

[156] Dyer, J., Gregersen, H., and Christensen, C. (2011). *The Innovator's DNA: Mastering the Five Skills of Disruptive Innovators*...ob. cit., p. 222.

[157] Sigafoos, R. (1983). *Absolutely, Positively Overnight!,* Memphis: St. Luke´s Press, 1983, p. 34. It's a translation from Spanish into English, not the exact words in Sigafoos.

[158] Ibídem.

[159] Duckworth, A. (2016). *Grit, The Power of Passion and Perseverance*, New York: Simon & Schuster, 2016, p. 9.

[160] "Jeff Dyer on Innovation" (2017). Available at: https://www.linkedin.com/learning/jeff-dyer-on-innovation.

[161] Lasorda, T. Available at: https://www.brainyquote.com/quotes/tommy_lasorda_139448.

[162] Sutton, R. (2010). *Good Boss, Bad Boss*, New York: Business Plus, p 38.

[163] Sutton, R. (2010). "The Delicate Art of Being Perfectly Assertive", Harvard Business Review, June 28, 2010.

[164] Cummings, A., and Oldham G. (1997). "Enhancing Creativity: Managing Work Contexts for the High Potential Employee", *California Management Review* 40 (1997): 22-38.

[165] Baard, P., Deci, E., and Ryan, R. (2004). "Intrinsic Need Satisfaction: A Motivational Basis of Performance and Well-Being in Two Work Settings," *Journal of Applied Social Psychology* 34 (2004).

[166] Kirton, M. J. (1989). *Adaptors and Innovators*, London, Routledge, 1989. Kirton, M. J. (1976). "Adaptors and Innovators: A Description and Measure," *Journal of Applied Psychology* 61 (1976): 622-29.

[167] Sutton, R. (2010). "Managing yourself: the Boss as a Human Shield", Harvard Business Review, September 2010.

[168] Sutton, R. (2002). *Weird Ideas That Work*, ob. cit., p. 179. William E. Coyne´s speech at Motorola University in Schaumburg, Illinois, July 11, 2000.

[169] Packard, D. (1995). *The HP Way: How Bill Hewlett and I Built Our Company*, New York: HarperBusiness, 1995, p. 108. Sutton, R. (2002). *Weird Ideas That Work*, ob. cit., p. 77.

[170] Rao, H., Sutton, R., and Webb A. (2008). "Innovation lessons from Pixar: An interview with Oscar-winning director Brad Bird", *McKinsey Quaterly*, April 2008. Available at: https://www.mckinsey.com. Sutton R. *Good Boss, Bad Boss*, ob. cit. p. 86.

[171] Sutton, R. (2010). *Good Boss, Bad Boss*, ob. cit. p. 87.

[172] Edmondson, A. C. (1999), "Psychological safety and learning behavior in work teams", *Administrative Science Quaterly*, 44, 350-383. Tucker, A. L., and Edmondson, A.C. (2003). "Why hospitals don´t learn from failures: Organizational and psychological dynamics that inhibit system change", *California Management Review*, 45, 55-72.

[173] Edmondson, A. C. (2004). "Learning From Mistakes Is Easier Said Than Done. Group and Organizational Influences on the Detection and Correction of Human Error", *The Journal of Applied Behavioral Science*, Vol. 40 No. 1, March 2004.

[174] Berkun, S. (2010). *The Myths of Innovation*, Sebastopol (Canadá): O`Reilly Media, 2010, p. 104.

[175] Isaacson, W. (2014). *Los innovadores, Los genios que inventaron el futuro*...ob. cit., p. 136.

[176] Drucker, P. (1987). *La innovación y el empresario innovador*, Buenos Aires: Sudamericana, 1987, p. 180.

[177] Ibidem, p. 186.

[178] Ibídem, p. 186.

[179] Duhigg, C. (2016). "What Google Learned From Its Quest to Build the Perfect Team", *The New York Times*, February 25, 2016.

[180] Woolley, A. et al.(2010). "Evidence for a Collective Intelligence Factor in the Performace of Human Groups", *Science*, Vol. 330, October 29, 2010.

[181] Rozovsky, J. (2015). "The five keys to a successful Google team", re Work, November 17, 2015. Available at: https://rework.withgoogle.com/blog/five-keys-to-a-successful-google-team/.

[182] Duhigg, C. (2016). "What Google Learned From Its Quest to Build the Perfect Team", *The New York Times*, February 25, 2016.

[183] Hofstede, G., Hofstede, G. J., and Minkow, M. (2010). *Culture and Organizations (Software of the Mind), Intercultural Cooperation and Its Importance for Survival*, United States, 2010, 3rd. ed.

[184] Barnett, H. (1953). *Innovation: The Basis of Cultural Change,* Nueva York, 1953, p. 65.

[185] Scott, S. (1992). "Why do some societies invent more than others?", *Journal of Business Venturing* 7, 29-46. Rinne, T., Steel, D., and Fairweather, J. (2012). "Hofstede and Shane Revisited: The Role of Power Distance and Individualism in National-Level Innovation Success", *Cross-Cultural Research 46 (2) 91-108, SAGE Publications*. Taylor, M. Z., and Wilson, S. (2012). "Does culture still matter?: The effects of individualism on national innovation rates", *Journal of Business Venturing* 27 (2012), 234-247.

[186] Isaacson, W. (2014). *Los innovadores*...ob. cit., p. 345 and p. 494 (translation from Spanish into English, not the exact words in Isaacson´s original book).

[187] Hofstede, G., Hofstede, G. J., and Minkow, M. (2010). *Culture and Organizations (Software of the Mind), Intercultural Cooperation and Its Importance for Survival*...ob. cit. pp. 57-59. Table 3.1 *Power Distance Index* (PDI).

[188] Ibidem, pp. 95-97. Table 4.1 *Individualism Index* (IDV).

[189] Dunning, D., Heath, C. ,and Suls, J. (2004). "Flawed Self-Assessment: Implications for Health, Education, and the Workplace,", *Psychological Science* 5 (2004): 69-106. Dunning, D. (2005). *Self-Insight*, New York, Psychology Press, 2005. Sutton, R. (2010). "Some Bosses Live in a Fool´s Paradise", Harvard Business Review, June 2, 2010.

[190] "Top 200 Jack Welch Quotes (2024 Update)", *QuoteFancy*. Available at: http://www.quotefancy.com. Sutton, R. *Good Boss, Bad Boss*, ob. cit. p. 245.

[191] Sutton, R. (2010). *Good Boss, Bad Boss*...ob. cit., p. 49. Weber, R. et al. (2001). "The Illusion of Leadership: Misattribution of Cause in Coordination Games", *Organization Science* 12, (2001): 582-598.

[192] Tiger, L. (1970). "Dominance in Human Societies", *Annual Review of Ecology and Systematics* 1 (1970): 298.

[193] A class with Robert Sutton. Eskridge, K. (2008). "They Watch Everything You Do,", *Humans at Work*, November 7, 2008. Available at: http://www.humansatwork.com.

[194] Bryant, A. (2009). "Linda Hudson of BAE on Fitting In, and Rising to the Top", *New York Times* (Corner Office) September 19, 2009.

[195] Keltner, D., Gruenfeld, D., and Anderson C. (2003). "Power, Approach, and Inhibition", *Psychological Review* 110 (2003): 265-284.

[196] "David Packard´s 11 Simple Rules", HP Retiree. Available at: http://www.hp.com/retiree/history/founders/packard/11rules.html.

[197] Amabile, T., and Kramer, S. (2011). *The Progress Principle: Using Small Wins to Ignite Joy, Engagement, and Creativity at Work*, Boston: Harvard Business School Publishing, 2011.

[198] Weick, K. E. (1984). "Small Wins: Redefining the Scale of Social Problems", *American Psychologist* 39 (1984): 40-49.

[199] Ibidem.

[200] Weick, K.E. (1984). "Small Wins: Redefining the Scale of Social Problems", ob. cit.

[201] Sutton, R. (2010). *Good Boss, Bad Boss*…ob. cit., p. 154.

[202] Mintzberg, H. (1990). "The Manager´s Jobs: Folklore and Fact", Harvard Business Review 68, no. 2 (1990): 165.

[203] "201 Amazing Steve Jobs Quotes (That Will Motivate You)". Available at: http://wisdomquotes.com/steve-jobs-quotes/.

[204] Sutton, R. (2011). "Pixar Lore: The Day Our Bosses Saved Our Jobs", Harvard Business Review, January 10, 2011.

[205] Mark G., Gonzalez, V., and Harris J. (2005). "No Task Left Behind? Examining the Nature of Fragmented Work" (paper, CHI 2005, Portland, OR, April 2-7, 2005), 113-120. Mark, G., Gudith, D., and Klocke, U. (2008). "The Cost of Interrupted Work: More Speed and Stress", in *Proceedings of the Twenty-Sixth Annual SIGCHI Conference on Human Factors in Computing Systems* (New York: ACM, 2008), 107-110.

[206] Rosoff, M. (2011): "Andreessen and Horowitz Charges Employees $10 Per Minute If They´re Late To Meetings", *Business Insider*, March 1, 2011.

[207] Bluedorn, A., Turban, D., and Love, M. (1999). "The Effects of Stand-Up and Sit-Down Meeting Formats on Meeting Outcomes", *Journal of Applied Psychology* 84 (1999): 277-285.

[208] Townsend, R. (2007). *Up the Organization*, San Francisco: Jossey-Bass, 2007, 1970, p. 130. Sutton, R. (2010). *Good Boss, Bad Boss*…ob. cit. p. 161.

[209] Sutton, R. (2010). *Good Boss, Bad Boss*…ob. cit. p. 161.

[210] A class with R. Sutton.

[211] Sellers, P. (2004). "P&G: Teaching An Old Dog New Tricks CEO A.G. Lafley has kicked up the good ideas at the stodgy Midwestern giant--and the company's growth too. Here's an inside look at how he's doing it." CNN Money, May 31, 2004.

212 Mossberg, W., and Swisher K. (2019). "Steve Jobs and Bill Gates Face Off". Available at: https://www.youtube.com/watch?v=Sw8x7ASpRIY&t=1286s.

213 Gaskins, R. (2012). "Viewpoint: How PowerPoint changed Microsoft and my life", BBC, July 31, 2012. Available at: www.bbc.com/news/technology.

214 Barr, J. (2015). "Doug Klunder '81 Excel creator works for civil liberties", *MIT Technology Review*, December 22, 2015. Available at: https://www.technologyreview.com/s/543961/doug-klunder-81/.

215 Edwards, B. (2011). "The iPod: How Apple's legendary portable music player came to be", Macworld, October 23, 2011. Available at: https://www.macworld.com/article/1163181/the-birth-of-the-ipod.html.

216 Hargadon, A. (2003). *How Breakthroughs Happen: The Surprising Truth About How Companies Innovate*...ob. cit., pp. 15-16.

217 Sala-i-Martin, X. (2017). "Economía en colores", Barcelona, p. 81. BrainyQuote. Available at https://www.brainyquote.com/quotes/isaac_newton_135885.

218 Fildes, J. (2007). "Darwin´s letters archive on web", BBC, May 16, 2007. Available at: http://news.bbc.co.uk/2/hi/science/nature/6657237.stm.

219 Hansen, M. (2009). *Collaboration*, Boston: Harvard Business School Publishing, 2009, p. 25.

220 Hansen, M. (2010). "IDEO CEO Tim Brown. T-Shaped Stars: The Backbone of IDEO's Collaborative Culture", Chief Excecutive, January 21, 2010. Available at: https://chiefexecutive.net/ideo-ceo-tim-brown-t-shaped-stars-the-backbone-of-ideoaes-collaborative-culture__trashed/.

221 A class with R. Sutton.

222 Sutton, R. (2010). *Good Boss, Bad Boss*...ob. cit., pp. 107-108.

223 "Microsoft´s Downfall: Inside the Executive E-Mails and Cannibalisti Culture that Felled a Tech Giant", *Vanity Fair*, July 3, 2012.

[224] Sutton, R. (2012). "Dysfunctional Internal Competition at Microsoft: we've seen the enemy, and it is us!", July 6, 2012. Available at: https://bobsutton.typepad.com/my_weblog/2012/07/dysfunctional-internal-competition-at-microsoft-weve-seen-the-enemy-and-it-is-us.html.

[225] Hansen, M. (2009). *Collaboration*...ob. cit., p 51.

[226] Ibidem, pp. 55-56.

[227] Tett, G. (2015). "Why the silo effect makes us stupid", *Financial Review*, August 28, 2015.

[228] Hansen, M. (2009). *Collaboration*...ob. cit., p. 7.

[229] Sellers, P. (2004). "P&G: Teaching An Old Dog New Tricks CEO A.G. Lafley has kicked up the good ideas at the stodgy Midwestern giant--and the company's growth too. Here's an inside look at how he's doing it." CNN Money, May 31, 2004.

[230] Cross, R., Rebele, R., and Grant, A. (2016). "Collaborative Overload", Harvard Business Review, January-February 2016.

[231] Kerr, S. (1995). "On the folly of rewarding A, while hoping for B", *Academy of Management Executive*, 1995, Vol. 9, No. 1.

[232] Hansen, M. (2009). *Collaboration*, ob. cit., p. 107.

[233] Goodall, J. (1988). *In the Shadow of Man*, New York, Houghton Mifflin, 1988. p. 6. Sutton, R. (2002). *Weird Ideas That Work*, New York: Free Press, p. 148.

[234] Karbo, K. (2019). "Jane Goodall, how a woman redefined mankind", *National Geographic*, January 18, 2019.

[235] Khun, T. (1970). *The Structure of Scientific Revolutions* (Second Edition, Enlarged), Thomas S. International Encyclopedia of Unified Science Volumes I and II-Foundations of the Unity of Science Volume II-Number 2, The University of Chicago Press, 1970, p. 90.

[236] Asakura, R. (2000). *Revolutionaries at Sony,* New York: McGraw-Hill, 2000, p. 229.

[237] McCarthy, D. (2008). "Fortune: The Best Advice I Ever Got", May 9, 2008. Great Leadership by Dan McCarthy, Available at: https://greatleadeshipbydan.com/.

[238] Hargadon, A. (2003). *How Breakthroughs Happen: The Surprising Truth About How Companies Innovate*…ob. cit., p. 86.

[239] Auletta, K. (2011). "A Woman´s Place", *The New Yorker,* July 4, 2011.

[240] "End of an Era: Google Executive Eric Schmidt to leave board", May 1, 2019, Brand&Leaders.com. Available at: https://www.brandsandleaders.com/2019/05/01/end-of-an-era-google-executive-eric-schmidt-to-leave-board/.

[241] Dyer J., Gregersen, H., and Christensen, C. (2011). *The Innovator's DNA: Mastering the Five Skills of Disruptive Innovators* …ob. cit., pp. 183-185.

[242] Ibidem, p. 188.

[243] Ibidem, p. 191.

[244] Ibidem, p. 228.

[245] Lashinsky, A. (2011). "How Apple Works: Inside the World's Biggest Startup", *Fortune,* May 9, 2011.

[246] Krantz, M. (2022). "13 Firms Hoard $1 Trillion In Cash (We're Looking At You Big Tech)", *Investors Business Daily*, February 3, 2022. Available at: https://www.investors.com/etfs-and-funds/sectors/sp500-companies-stockpile-1-trillion-cash-investors-want-it/.

[247] Lashinsky, A. (2011). "How Apple Works: Inside the World's Biggest Startup", *Fortune,* May 9, 2011.

[248] A class with Robert Sutton.

[249] Sutton, R. (2014). "Why Big Teams Suck: Seven (Plus or Minus Two) is the Magical Number Once Again". Available at: https://bobsutton.typepad.com/my_weblog/2014/03/why-big-teams-suck-seven-plus-or-minus-two-is-the-magical-number-once-again.html.

[250] Ibidem.

[251] A class with Robert Sutton.

[252] Messick, D., and Kramer, R. (2005). *The Psychology of Leadership: New Perspectives and Research*, New York: Psychology Press, 2005, p. 126.

[253] Eisenhardt, K., and Schoonhoven, C. (1990). "Organizational Growth: Linking Founding Team, Strategy, Environment, and Growth Among U.S. Semiconductor Ventures, 1978-1988", *Administrative Science Quarterly* 35 (1990): 504-529.

[254] Hackman, R. (2002). *Leading Teams*, Boston: Harvard Business School Press, 2002, pp. 54-59.

[255] "Ruining it for the Rest of Us", *This American Life*, episode 370, December 19, 2008. Available at: https://www.thisamericanlife.org/370/ruining-it-for-the-rest-of-us. Felps W., Mitchell, T., and Byington, E. (2006). "How, When, And Why Bad Apple Spoil the Barrel: Negative Group Members and Dysfunctional Groups", *Research in Organizational Behavior*, Volume 27, 175-222 (2006).

[256] Sutton, R. (2010). *Good Boss, Bad Boss*...ob. cit., p. 100.

[257] A class with R. Sutton.

[258] Vohs, K., Baumeister, R., Bratslavsky, E., and Finkenauer C. (2001). "Bad is Stronger Than Good", *Review of General Psychology*, 2001, Vol. 5, No. 4, 323-370.

[259] Ibidem.

[260] Ibidem.

261 Andersen, E. (2013). "21 Quotes From Henry Ford On Business, Leadership And Life", *Forbes*, May 31, 2013.

262 "How Elon Musk has missed his targets on delivering affordable cars", *Reuters*, March 1, 2023.

263 Rao H., Sutton R., and Webb, A. P. (2008). "Innovation lessons from Pixar: An interview with Oscar-winning director Brad Bird" ob. cit. Snell J. "5 Walt Disney Inspiring Quotes", October 1, 2018. Available at: https://www.news.disney.com.

264 Rosenthal, R., and Rubin, D. B. (1978). "Interpersonal Expectancy Effects: The First 345 Studies", *Behavioral and Brain Sciences* 3 (1978): 377-86. Rosenthal, R., and Jacobson, L. (1968). *Pygmalion in the Classroom: Teacher Expectations and Pupils' Intellectual Development* (New York: Holt, Rinehart & Winston, 1968). Livingston, J.S. (1969). "Pygmalion in Management", *Harvard Business Review* 47 (1969): 81-89. Eden, D., (1984). "Self-Fulfilling Prophecy as a Management Tool: Harnessing Pygmalion" *Academy of Management Review* 9 (1984): 64-73.

265 Eden, D., and Shani, A. (1982). "Pygmalion Goes to Boot Camp: Expectancy, Leadership and Trainee Performance", *Journal of Applied Psychology* 67 (1982): 194-199.

266 A class with Robert Sutton.

267 Martin, L., and Delgado, M. (2011). "The Influence of Emotional State on Decision-Making Under Risk", *J Cogn Neurosci* 2011 Sep;23(9):2569-81.doi: 10.1162/jocn.2011.21618. Epub 2011 Jan 21.

268 Gardner, N. (2006). "Emotionally ambivalent workers are more creative, innovative", University of Washington, October 5, 2006. Available at: http://www.washington.edu/news/2006/10/05/emotionally-ambivalent-workers-are-more-creative-innovative/. Fong, C. T. (2006). "The Effects of Emotional Ambivalence on Creativity", *The Academy of Management Journal*, Vol. 49, No. 5 (October, 2006), pp. 1016-1030.

269 Hatfield, E., Cacioppo, J., and Rapson, R. (1994). *Emotional Contagion* (Cambridge, UK: Cambridge University Press, 1994). Colligan, M. (1982).

Pennebaker, J. y Murphy, L., *Mass Psychogenic Illness: A Social Psychological Analysis* (Hillsdale, NJ: Erlbaum, 1982).

[270] Sutton, R. (2010). *Good Boss, Bad Boss*...ob.cit., p. 120.

[271] A class with Robert Sutton.

[272] Vohs, K., Mead, N., and Goode, M. (2006). "The Psychological Consequences of Money", *Science*, Vol. 314, No. 5802, (November 17, 2006), pp. 1154-1156.

[273] Lashinsky, A. (2011). "How Apple Works: Inside the World's Biggest Startup", *Fortune*, 9 de mayo de 2011. Deutschman, A. (2000). "The once and future Steve Jobs", October 11, 2000. Available at: http://www.salon.com/technology/books/2000/10/11/jobs_excerpt.

[274] Rao, H., Sutton, R., and Webb, A. (2008). "Innovation lessons from Pixar: An interview with Oscar-winning director Brad Bird", ob. cit.

[275] Lashinsky, A. (2011). "How Apple Works: Inside the World's Biggest Startup", *Fortune*, May 9, 2011.

[276] Steve Jobs: speech at Stanford University June 12, 2005. Available at: https://news.stanford.edu/2005/06/14/jobs-061505/.

[277] "Annacone, el guía espiritual de Sampras y Federer", *La Nación*, Buenos Aires, August 1, 2019.

[278] Zenger, J., Folkman, J., and Edinger, S. (2009). "How Extraordinary Leaders Double Profits", *Chief Learning Officer*, julio de 2009. Kirkland, R. ed., *What Matters? Ten Questions That Will Shape Our Future* (McKinsey Management Institute, 2009), 80.

[279] Bick, J. (2007). "The Google Way: Give Engineers Room", *New York Times*, October 21, 2007.

[280] Pink, D. (2009). *Drive, The Surprising Truth About What Motivates Us*...ob. cit., p. 99.

[281] Ibidem, p. 91.

[282] Ibidem, pp. 42-43.

[283] Deci, E., Koestner, R., and Ryan, R. (2001). "Extrinsic Rewards and Intrinsic Motivation in Education: Reconsidered Once Again", *Review of Education Research* 71, no. 1(Spring 2001): 14.

[284] Pink, D. (2009). *Drive, The Surprising Truth About What Motivates Us*...ob. cit., pp. 13-14.

[285] Sutton, R. (2010). *Good Boss, Bad Boss*...ob. cit. p. 85.

[286] Sutton, R. (2010). "It´s Up to You to Start a Good Fight", Harvard Business Review, August 3, 2010.

[287] Catmull, E., and Wallacem A. (2014). "Creativity, Inc.: Overcoming the Unseen Forces That Stand in the Way of True Inspiration". Available at: https://highlights.sawyerh.com/volumes/a1351c21-deba-45a0-9ec2-6322200c1753.

[288] Sutton, R. (2010). "It´s Up to You to Start a Good Fight", Harvard Business Review, ob. cit.

[289] Sutton, R. "Fight Like You're Right, Listen Like You're Wrong and Other Keys to Great Management", *First Round Review, Management*. Available at: https://firstround.com/review/Fight-Like-Youre-Right-Listen-Like-Youre-Wrong-and-Other-Keys-to-Great-Management/.

[290] "Disagree and Commit: The Importance of disagreement in decision making", HackerNoon, January 17, 2019. Available at: https://hackernoon.com.

[291] Lopez Rosetti, D. (2017). *Emoción y sentimientos*, Buenos Aires, Planeta, 2017. Bachrach, E. (2012). *Ágil mente*, Buenos Aires, Sudamericana, 2012, pp. 86-87.

[292] Kotter, J., and Cohen, D. (2002). *The Heart of Change*, Boston, Harvard Business Review Press.

[293] Damasio, A. (2003). *El error de Descartes*, Buenos Aires, Paidós, p. 10.

[294] Ibidem, p. 71.

[295] Bachrach, E. (2012). *EnCambio*, Buenos Aires, Sudamericana, p. 396.

[296] Isen, A. M., Daubman, K. A., and Nowicki, G. P. (1987). "Positive Affect Facilitates Creative Problem Solving", *Journal of Personality and Social Psychology*, Vol. 52: 1122-1131. Isen, A. M. et. al. (1985). "The Influence of Positive Affect on Clinical Problem Solving", *Medical Decision Making* 11:221-227.

[297] Nyberg, A. et al. (2009). "Managerial Leadership and Ischaemic Heart Disease Among Employees: The Swedish WOLF Study", *Occupational and Environmental Medicine* 66 (2009): 51-55.

[298] Sutton, R., and Rao, H. (2014). *Scalling Up Excellence*, ob. cit., p. 82.

[299] Ibidem, p. 83.

[300] Ibidem, p. 84.

[301] A class with Huggy Rao. McBride, E. (2014). "Slam the Clam: Lesson From BP's Fast Growth", *Forbes*, October 31, 2014. "Hayagreeva Rao Keynote Talk: Scaling Up Excellence at Stanford GSB", The Singju Post, February 29, 2016. Availlable at: https://singjupost.com.

[302] Sutton, R., and Rao, H. (2014). *Scalling Up Excellence*..ob. cit., pp. 79-80.

[303] Ibidem, p. 81.

[304] A class with Sutton, R. Lafley, A. G., and Charan, R. (2008). *Game Changer*, New York, Random House, p. 21.

[305] Sutton, R. (2010). *Good Boss, Bad Boss*...ob. cit., p. 128.

[306] Ibidem, p. 93.

[307] Ibidem, p. 135.

[308] Ibidem, p. 179.

[309] "Communication: Keep it Simple", Leading Blog: A Leadership Blog". Available at: https://www.leadershipnow.com/leadingblog/2008/10/communication_keep_it_simple.html.

[310] Sutton, R. (2010). *Good Boss, Bad Boss*…ob. cit., p. 145.

[311] Shneider, A. (2010). "Chocolate Cake v. Fruit Or Why Get Emotional During 'Rational' Negotiations", January 26, 2010. Available at: Indisputably Blog, indisputably.org/2010/01.

[312] Sutton, R. (2010). *Good Boss, Bad Boss*…ob. cit., p. 146.

[313] Sutton, R. (2010). *Good Boss, Bad Boss*…ob. cit., pp. 77-78.

[314] Bezos quote. "Quotefancy". Available at: https://quotefancy.com/quote/1093142/Jeff-Bezos-If-you-want-to-be-inventive-you-have-to-be-willing-to-fail.

[315] Lafley, A. G., and Charan, R. (2008). *Game Changer*, New York, Random House, 2008, p. 21. Dyer, J, and Gregersen, H. "Frequently Asked Questions About The Innovation Premium", *Forbes*, August 14, 2013.

[316] Hargadon, A. (2003). *How Breakthroughs Happen: The Surprising Truth About How Companies Innovate*…ob. cit., p. 93.

[317] Cross, R., Baker, W., and Parker, A. (2003). "What creates energy in organizations?", *MITSloan Management Review*, June, 2003. Sutton, R. (2010). *Good Boss, Bad Boss*…ob. cit., p. 109.

[318] Design Shangai (2023). "The Slow Death of Design", Stories, 16-11-2023, Available at: https://design.shangai/stories.

[319] "Triumph of the Nerds 1995", all about Steve Jobs. Available at: https://allaboutstevejobs.com/videos/misc/triumph_of_the_nerds_interview_1995.

[320] "IDEO founder David Kelley talks design, Steve Jobs, cancer, and the importance of empathy", 9to5Mac, Weintraub, S., 6 de enero de 2013.

Available at: https://9to5mac.com/2013/01/06/ideo-founder-david-kelley-talks-design-steve-jobs-cancer-and-the-importance-of-empathy/.

[321] "IDEO founder David Kelley talks design, Steve Jobs, cancer, and the importance of empathy", 9to5Mac, Weintraub, S., 6 de enero de 2013. Available at: https://9to5mac.com/2013/01/06/ideo-founder-david-kelley-talks-design-steve-jobs-cancer-and-the-importance-of-empathy/.

[322] About IDEO, https://www.ideo.com/about. Hargadon, A. (2003). *How Breakthroughs Happen: The Surprising Truth About How Companies Innovate*...ob. cit., p. 136.

[323] Hargadon, A. (2003). *How Breakthroughs Happen: The Surprising Truth About How Companies Innovate*...ob. cit., pp. 141-148.

[324] IDEO, "Designing a School System from the Ground Up". Available at: https://www.ideo.com/case-study/designing-a-school-system-from-the-ground-up. Claire, M. (2014). "Shaping a School System from the Ground Up", *The New York Times*, July 5, 2014.

[325] "Seis atributos innovadores que debe tener una organización para no desaparecer", *Infobae*, June 25, 2019. "Como lograr estos 6 atributos que poseen las empresas mas innovadoras del mundo", *El Cronista*, June 19, 2019. "Ideo Studied Innovation In 100+ Companies–Here's What It Found", *Fast Company*, March 20, 2017. Tang, S., and Aycan, D. (2018). "How to Set the Conditions for Innovation", IDEO, July 6, 2018. Available at: https://www.ideo.com/search?q=Creative%20Difference.

[326] IDEO-Tools: "Creative Difference: A Customized Guide to a More Innovative and Adaptive Culure". Available at: https://www.ideo.com/post/creative-difference.

[327] Kelley, T., and Kelley, D. (2013). *Creative Confidence*, ob. cit. p. 41.

[328] Ibidem, p. 130.

[329] Ibidem, p. 141.

[330] Ibidem, p. 143.

[331] Salter, S. (2008). "Marissa Mayer´s 9 Principles of Innnovation", *FastCompany*, 2-19-2008.

[332] Stewart, K. (2007). "The Institutional Yes", Harvard Business Review, October, 2007.

[333] Kelley, T. , and Kelley, D. (2013). *Creative Confidence*…ob. cit. ,p. 186.

[334] Yamashita, K. (IDEO). *From Superpowers to Great Teams* in IDEO University. Available at: https://www.ideou.com/products/leading-for-creativity.

[335] Brown, J. (IDEO): *The Power of Purpose* in IDEO University. Available at: https://www.ideou.com/pages/course-calendar.

[336] Neighmond, P. (2014). "People Who Feel They Have A Purpose In Life Live Longer", NPR, July 28, 2014. Available at: https://www.npr.org/sections/health-shots/2014/07/28/334447274/people-who-feel-they-have-a-purpose-in-life-live-longer.

[337] Grant, A. (2010). "Putting a Face to a Name: The Art of Motivating Employees", Wharton, University of Pennsylvania, Management, February, 17 2010,. Available at: https://knowledge.wharton.upenn.edu/article/putting-a-face-to-a-name-the-art-of-motivating employees/. Leadership Foundry, "Do You Know How to RETAIN TALENT?. Available at: https://www.leadershipfoundry.com/retain-talent/.

[338] Brown, J. (IDEO): *The Power of Purpose* in IDEO University. Available at: https://www.ideou.com/pages/course-calendar.

[339] Hirsch, J. y Hsu, T. (2014). "Elon Musk opens up Tesla patents; it 'isn't entirely altruistic", *Los Angeles Times*, June 12, 2014.

[340] Sinek S. "How Great Leaders Inspire Action". Available at: https://www.ted.com/talks/simon_sinek_how_great_leaders_inspire_action?language=en. "Transcript for Simon Sinek: How great leaders inspire action" Also available at: BYU-Idaho. https://brightspotcdn.byui.edu/f7/15/ad478c304f07b48327e9d9dcd6fb/ponder-spiel-joseph-smiths-lessons.pdf.

341 Bennis, W., and Namus, B. (1985). *Leaders: The Strategies for Taking Charge*, Harpercollins, 1985. US Army Heritage and Education Center. Q. Who first originated the term VUCA (Volatility, Uncertainty, Complexity and Ambiguity)?. Available at: https://usawc.libanswers.com/faq/84869.

342 Scott, D. A., Viguerie, P., Schwartz, E. y Van Landeghem, J. (2018): "2018 Corporate Longevity Forecast: Creative Destruction is Accelerating", *Innosight*, 6 de febrero de 2018. Available at: https://www.innosight.com/insight/creative-destruction.

343 Pandey, E. (2018). "How Barnes & Noble, the last big bookstore, fell to Amazon", *Axios*, October 7, 2018.

344 Lambert, F. (2022). "Tesla still dominates US electric car market, and it´s not even closs", *Electrek*, March 17, 2022.

345 "Microsoft's Kevin Scott & Kathleen Hogan discuss Bay Area presence & careers", *The Official Microsoft Blog*, February, 28 2019. Available at: https://blogs.microsoft.com/bayarea/2019/02/28/microsoft-growth-conference-kevin-scott-kathleen-hogan/

346 Wentz, R. C. (2012). *The Innovation Machine*...ob. cit. p. 176 (chapter 6.3. *BMW is a Master of Idea Sourcing*).

347 Kelley, T., and Kelley, D. (2013). *Creative Confidence* ..ob. cit. pp. 208-209.

348 "A Dozen Things I've Learned from Marissa Mayer about Business, Management, and Innovation", 25ip, December 14, 2014. Available at: https://25ip.com/2014.

349 Isen, A. M., Daubman, K. A., and Nowicki, G. P. (1987). "Positive Affect Facilitates Creative Problem Solving", *Journal of Personality and Social Psychology*, Vol. 52: 1122-1131. Isen, A. M. et. al. (1985). "The Influence of Positive Affect on Clinical Problem Solving", *Medical Decision Making* 11:221-227.

350 Shane, S. (1992). "Why do some societies invent more than others?", *Journal of Business Venturing* 7, 29-46. Rinne, T., Steel, D., and Fairweather, J. (2012). "Hofstede and Shane Revisited: The Role of Power Distance and Individualism in National-Level Innovation Success", *Cross-Cultural Research*

46 (2) 91-108, SAGE Publications. Taylor, M. Z., and Wilson, S. (2012). "Does culture still matter?: The effects of individualism on national innovation rates", *Journal of Business Venturing* 27 (2012), 234-247.

www.ingramcontent.com/pod-product-compliance
Lightning Source LLC
Chambersburg PA
CBHW071915210526
45479CB00002B/429